Guitar
Chords

Guitar Chords

150 Essential Guitar Chords

Ted Fuller & Julian Hayman

METRO BOOKS
New York

METRO BOOKS
New York

An Imprint of Sterling Publishing
1166 Avenue of the Americas
New York, NY 10036

METRO BOOKS and the distinctive Metro Books logo are trademarks
of Sterling Publishing Co., Inc.

ARTWORK CREDITS
All pictures © Amber Books except for the following:
6(l): Getty Images/Dorling Kindersley; 6(r): Corbis/Bob Jacobson; 7: Bridgeman Art Library/
Roger-Viollet/Bibliotheque Nationale; 10: Getty Images/March of Time/Time Life Pictures;
11(t): Getty Images/Michael Ochs Archives; 11(bl): Fender; 11(bc): Gibson;
11(br): Rickenbacker; 12: Corbis/Lynn Goldsmith; 13: Corbis/Neal Preston.

Editorial and design by
Amber Books Ltd
74–77 White Lion Street
London N1 9PF
www.amberbooks.co.uk

Project Editor: Sarah Uttridge
Design: Zoe Mëllors

ISBN: 978-1-4351-5860-3

For information about custom editions, special sales, and premium and corporate purchases,
please contact Sterling Special Sales at 800-805-5489 or specialsales@sterlingpublishing.com.

Manufactured in China

2 4 6 8 10 9 7 5 3 1

www.sterlingpublishing.com

CONTENTS

Introduction

Instruments similar to the guitar have existed in some form for about 5000 years. The guitar is thought to have developed from early instruments in India and Central Asia. The oldest known instrument that shares the main features of a guitar was seen in a stone carving some 3300 years old, which shows a Hittite bard. The word 'guitar' came into the English language via the Indian instrument, sitar, journeying through Persia and Greece, and finally arriving in Spain as the 'guitarra'.

The Middle Ages and Renaissance stretched over more than a thousand years, from the end of the Western Roman Empire to the beginning of the seventeenth century, and the foundations of Western music were laid in place during this long period.

EARLY GUITARS

Music was played on a vast array of instruments during the medieval period. Many of these still exist today, and although they are made of different materials, such as silver or other metals rather than wood, they retain many of the same characteristics.

The recorder is an instrument that was used in medieval times and which has pretty much retained its original form. Stringed instruments that were plucked were used extensively in medieval music, such as the lute, gittern and mandora.

The guitar as we know it today can be traced back to the fifteenth century and is from the area around Malaga in southern Spain. This early version looked more like a ukulele

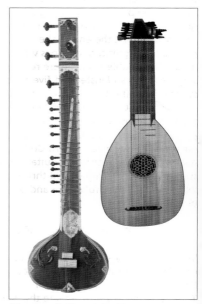

The sitar (left) and the European lute (right) are both early instruments that were played by being plucked.

and was much smaller than modern guitars. It had four pairs of strings and each set of strings was called a course.

Throughout the period of the Renaissance, the lute enjoyed far more respect than the guitar, which was never considered as a serious instrument. However, the guitar began to grow in popularity as more pieces became available and publications included articles about guitar technique.

During the Baroque period, which started around the turn of the seventeenth century, there were dramatic developments in art and music. It was during this period that a fifth course of strings was added to the guitar, which gave the pieces being written added complexity and helped to increase the popularity of the guitar greatly as people's tastes became more sophisticated. At the end of the Baroque period, two significant changes were made. The double strings were replaced by single strings, and instead of five pairs of strings the guitar had six single strings.

During the Classical period that followed, many composers and performers for the guitar began to

Fernando Sor helped to elevate the guitar to a concert instrument.

emerge. Fernando Sor, Mauro Guilliani, Fernando Carulli and others wrote music, published articles on guitar technique and performed concerts. Soon the guitar's popularity spread throughout Europe and to the United States, where seeds of the folk, rock and blues guitar techniques we use today would be sown.

POLYPHONY AND THE START OF MUSICAL NOTATION

Vocal polyphony – music for many voices – began during the ninth century, creating beautiful music from voices that interwove with each other. Polyphony was really the start of composition as we know it today. The motet and conductus were the main polyphonic forms of the early Middle Ages. Music was almost exclusively heard in church, but wandering musicians provided entertainment by singing long, narrative songs. Polyphony was not written in a major or minor key but in sections of one diatonic scale.

Plainsong, which is also known as plainchant, is a body of traditional songs used in the liturgies of the Roman Catholic and Anglican churches. Once the forms of service were well established, musicians started to experiment by embellishing the original melodies and added extra parts to make them more ornate.

MODERN MUSICAL NOTATION

Musical notation has steadily become much more developed and sophisticated, these days the slightest change in key, timings, and even emphasis is notated to give the player a clear understanding of what the composer was trying to convey when the piece was written. Guitarists today use major, minor, suspended and diminshed chords, and even alter the tuning of the guitar to add variety and colour to their music.

MAJOR SCALE

The major scale is made up of tones and semitones arranged in a certain order. There is an interval of a semitone between the third and fourth, and seventh and eighth degrees, and a tone between any other two adjacent notes.
   This is the scale of C.

Doh	Ray	Me	Fah	So	Lah	Te	Doh
1	2	3	4	5	6	7	8
C	D	E	F	G	A	B	C

MINOR SCALE

The minor scale is often chosen by composers to convey sad or expressive music, although there are many examples of this in major keys. The sad effect is due to the flattened third scale, which gives the minor scale its character. This is the natural scale of A minor: A B C D E F G A.
   A simple way to remember the steps in the natural minor scale is to start on the sixth degree of the relative major scale. This means that you do not have to learn a new set of steps, just the familiar major scale steps with a different starting point. For example, A is the sixth scale note of the C major scale, so the A natural minor scale is just the C major scale starting on the sixth scale note.

SIMPLE CHORD CONSTRUCTIONS

Chords are combinations of three or more musical pitches. They are constructed based on the notes in the major scale. The simplest chord is a major chord and all other chords are derived from the major chord. It is quite simple to stick with the key of C because it has no sharps or flats. Chords follow up the scale, skipping in steps of two.

Major

To make the chord of C major, start with the first note C. Then, skipping up by twos, add the third and fifth notes. Thus the chord of C is made up of the following notes: C, E, G.

Minor

A minor chord is a major chord with a flattened third note, or the third note played down one semitone (i.e. one fret). So, if we were to play the chord of C minor, we would use the notes C, E flat, G.

Diminished

To make a diminished chord, add a flat to the fourth and fifth notes of the chord. Using C major as our starting point: our chord is C, E flat, G flat. By adding a sharp to the fifth note, you get an augmented chord: C, E, G sharp.

Suspended

There are only two other traditional three-note chords, and they are both forms of the suspended chord. They replace the third with either a second or a fourth. Therefore, C sus 2 would be C, D, G. C sus 4 would be C, F, G.

Four-note chords

Four-note chords are simply triads with one note added to give a more colourful sound. Using the scale shown above, a C major seventh chord is C, E, G, B. If you see C maj 7, play C, E, G, B; if you see C7, flatten the seventh note, making the chord C, E, G, B flat.

USING CHORDS FOR DIFFERENT EFFECTS

To add interest to your compositions, be adventurous and try using chords you are not quite so familiar with.

As well as the sad and expressive quality of minor chords, many songwriters use minor chords to add interest, or during the middle eight of a song. If you're writing a song, try experimenting with one or two minor chords to see which one fits.

Major sevenths are an ideal ingredient for a jazzy and slightly mysterious feel, minors for a folky or sadder sound. Use suspended chords in pop songs and resolve them into a major chord. Use barre chords to get extra drive and a bass sound into your music. Try Am (add 9) for an '80s or Gothic feel, or major sixths for a Beatles feel.

The possibilities are endless. It's great fun to experiment with well-known chords and also to find some chords by accident. After all, if a chord sounds right and you are not actually sure what it is called, does that really matter?

GUITAR INNOVATORS

More recent innovators on the guitar include Leadbelly, born in 1888. He was a multi-instrumentalist but became famous for the driving rhythmic sound he got by using a 12-string guitar. Leadbelly directly influenced Woody Guthrie, with whom he played.

Two guitarists who would have a huge influence on folk guitarists in the 1960s were Elizabeth Cotton and Rev. Gary Davis, who were both born in the

1890s. Cotton fused elements of the dance tunes, rags, and hymns that she'd heard growing up. She developed a lovely, finger-picking style, which was later copied by many people, including Peter, Paul and Mary. The Rev. Gary Davis was famed for a more complex style that included a mix of ragtime and gospel influences.

Robert Johnson, born in 1911, was an American blues guitarist. Johnson used the bass strings of the guitar to produce an alternating bass sound. He died when he was only 27, but his few treasured recordings became the basis of the blues guitar sound.

Multi-instrumentalist Leadbelly with his 12-string acoustic guitar.

Django Reinhardt relearned to play guitar after his third and fourth fingers were partially paralyzed.

Born just one year before Johnson on the other side of the Atlantic in Belgium, Django Reinhardt was one of a number of gypsy guitarists playing in Europe at the time. Although Reinhardt did not read or write words or music, he developed an extraordinary instrumental technique. This was despite the loss of use of the two middle fingers on his left hand, which were badly burned in a fire in the caravan where he lived.

Woody Guthrie used old folk tunes that had been passed down, and constructed new songs with lyrics protesting about poverty and injustice. Players like Guthrie and Leadbelly were a huge influence on Bob Dylan and the legions of protest songwriters and folk singers that came out of America in the '60s.

ELECTRIC GUITARS, AMPLIFIERS, EFFECTS AND THE FUTURE

The arrival of amplification in the big-band era of the late 1920s and '30s would take electric guitar playing in all sorts of fascinating directions. The very first

After the introduction of the Fender Telecaster (left), the Gibson Les Paul (middle) was developed. Far right is the Rickenbacker.

electric guitars were simply archtop acoustic guitar bodies to which electromagnetic transducers had been attached. These were necessary to compete with the loud volume levels from the big-band brass sections.

The first manufactured electric guitar was by Rickenbacker in the 1930s, but the popular forms that are still used today were brought in by Fender and Gibson during the 1950s.

The earliest guitar amplifiers were probably simple audio amplifiers, but the electric guitar and its amplification quickly developed a life of its own, supported by specialist manufacturers.

A later generation of blues players, including T-Bone Walker, B. B. King, John Lee Hooker and Muddy Waters, would utilize the increased volume the electric guitar offered them in their playing. The use of electric instruments was key in rock guitar too, and a new style was emerging, one that was invented by Chuck Berry. Fusing blues and country, Berry created a deceptively simple style, which is still copied by rock guitarists today.

A younger generation of guitarists who were brought up listening to the early blues and rock 'n' roll players would use amplification in a previously unthinkable way and start to push the guitar to new limits. Guitar effects pedals began to hit on the market, and would enhance or completely change the sound of the guitar.

Jimi Hendrix used wah-wah and fuzz pedals; he also turned his amplifier up to

Chuck Berry comes the closest of any single figure to being the one who invented rock 'n' roll.

ear-splitting levels to create distortion and feedback. Rock guitarists like the Who's Pete Townshend and Jimmy Page of Led Zeppelin took rock 'n' roll and blues styles and cranked them right up, using pedals and stacks of amplification.

So, the guitar continues to develop, with new guitar heroes steadily replacing the old guard. Jack White from the White Stripes uses folk blues, show tunes and Jimmy Page-style riffs to create music that sounds utterly contemporary. Alex Turner and the Arctic Monkeys have created an interlocking riff machine that inspires and excites young players, but bears little or no resemblance to the music of those early guitar pioneers.

Jimmy Page was named 'Guitarist of the Year' five years in a row during the 1970s by Creem *magazine.*

A

The A major chord has a big, positive sound and is one of the
first chords many guitarists learn. Folk and country players
often add interest by moving between this chord,
Asus4 and Asus2 (simply remove the ring finger
and let the open B string sound).

A

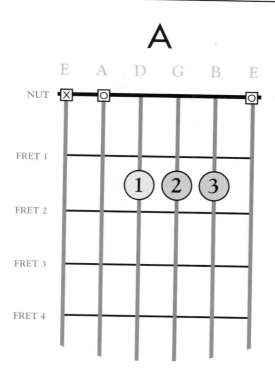

| ☐ | = OPEN STRING | ☒ | = DO NOT PLAY THIS STRING | ◯ | = OPTIONAL NOTE |

Your index finger should play the 2nd fret of the D string, while your middle finger plays the 2nd fret of the G string and your ring finger plays the 2nd fret of the B string.

A (alt. shape)

This alternative to a basic A chord is great if you're playing
with another player and you want to add a 'chiming' second
guitar part. Try decorating the chord by adding your
little finger at the 7th fret, top E string, resulting in an
alternative A(add9) shape.

A (alt. shape)

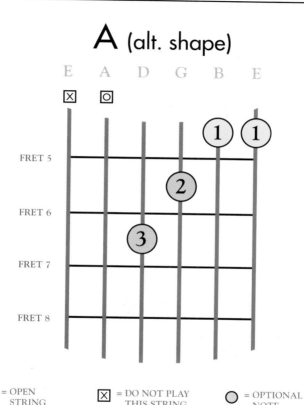

FRET 5

FRET 6

FRET 7

FRET 8

☐ = OPEN STRING   ☒ = DO NOT PLAY THIS STRING   ⬤ = OPTIONAL NOTE

You can also play the A chord by using your index finger on the 5th frets of the top E and B strings, your middle finger to play the 6th fret of the G string and your ring finger to play the 7th fret of the D string.

A(add9)

This classic pop chord is quite a stretch in most keys,
but the open A and E strings make it a little easier in A.
Try arpeggiating the notes and transport yourself
straight back to 1983!

A(add9)

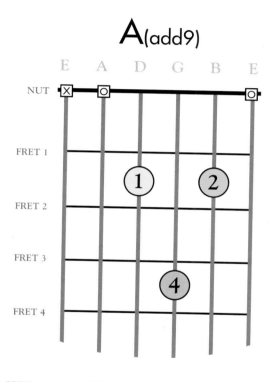

E   A   D   G   B   E

NUT

FRET 1

FRET 2

FRET 3

FRET 4

☉ = OPEN STRING   ☒ = DO NOT PLAY THIS STRING   ⬤ = OPTIONAL NOTE

The index finger plays the D string, 2nd fret. The second finger plays the B string, 2nd fret. The little finger plays the G string, 4th fret. The A and top E strings are open.

Seventh chords are an essential ingredient in blues and jazz. This easy A7 shape works well with D7 and E7 if you want to play the blues in A.

A7

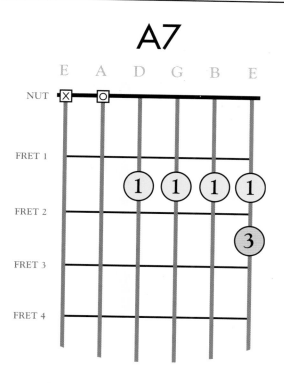

E   A   D   G   B   E

NUT

FRET 1

FRET 2

FRET 3

FRET 4

☐ = OPEN STRING   ☒ = DO NOT PLAY THIS STRING   ◯ = OPTIONAL NOTE

Use your index finger across the 2nd frets of the top E, B, G and D strings only, then use your middle or your ring finger, whichever feels most comfortable, to play the G note at the 3rd fret of the top E string.

AMAJOR7

Major seventh chords sound jazzy and slightly mysterious.
Like most open A chords, this one is easy to play.
If you're in the key of A and changing from this
to a D or Dmaj7 chord, an A7 chord in between
works rather well.

AMAJOR7

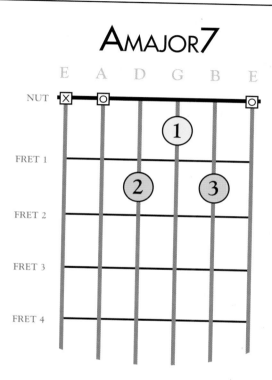

E   A   D   G   B   E

NUT

FRET 1

FRET 2

FRET 3

FRET 4

☐ = OPEN STRING   ☒ = DO NOT PLAY THIS STRING   ○ = OPTIONAL NOTE

Use your index finger to play the 1st fret of the G string, your middle finger to play the 2nd fret of the D string and finally your ring finger to play the 2nd fret of the B string.

Am

The open A minor chord has a folky and slightly sad sound.
Finger-picking works well with this shape; for a really
mysterious vibe, try moving the fretted notes up two frets
while leaving the open strings as they are.

Am

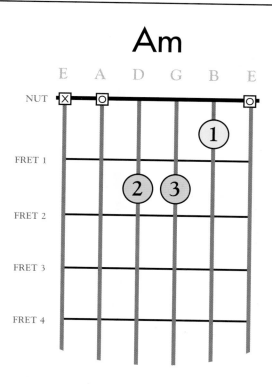

E	A	D	G	B	E

☐ = OPEN STRING   ☒ = DO NOT PLAY THIS STRING   ⬤ = OPTIONAL NOTE

Using your index finger, play the C note at the 1st fret of the B string, while your middle finger plays the 2nd fret of the D string and your ring finger plays the 2nd fret of the G string.

Am (alt. shape)

Another highly useful and relatively easy barre chord shape.
The full barre makes this chord completely moveable.
For a 'classical' sound, try leaving the low E string open
before going to E7 and then back to a standard Am chord.

Am (alt. shape)

E   A   D   G   B   E

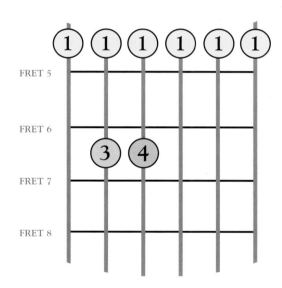

| FRET 5 |
| FRET 6 |
| FRET 7 |
| FRET 8 |

◻ = OPEN STRING   ☒ = DO NOT PLAY THIS STRING   ◯ = OPTIONAL NOTE

Using your index finger, play across all six strings of the 5th fret. Your ring finger should play the 7th fret of the A string and your little finger should play the 7th fret of the D string.

Am(add9)

The minor (add 9) chord sounds slightly gothic and was much beloved of moody '80s rock bands. This open version is relatively easy, though the little finger has quite a stretch – easier on electric than acoustic!

Am(add9)

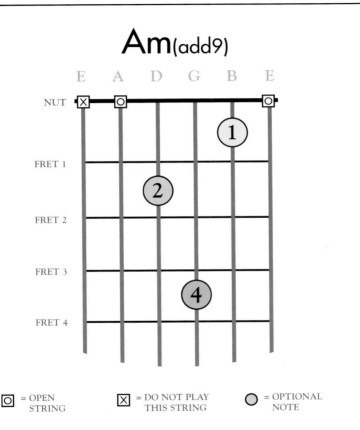

☐ = OPEN STRING   ☒ = DO NOT PLAY THIS STRING   ⬤ = OPTIONAL NOTE

The index finger plays the B string, 1st fret. The middle finger plays the D string, 2nd fret, and the little finger plays the G string, 4th fret. The A and top E strings are open.

Am7

A very easy shape; minor seventh chords sound slightly jazzy. This one sounds great after a C or Cmaj7 chord (moving through Dm7 and then G7 completes a sequence found in many jazz, Latin and pop songs).

Am7

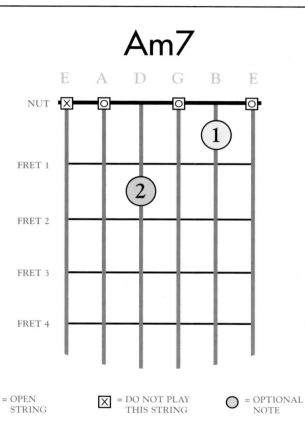

⊡ = OPEN STRING   ☒ = DO NOT PLAY THIS STRING   ◯ = OPTIONAL NOTE

Let your index finger play the 1st fret of the B string and your middle finger the 2nd fret of the D string. You should play all the other strings, except the bottom E, open.

31

Asus4

This chord has a 'chiming' sound that has made it a favourite
of singer/songwriters. Suspended chords sound as though
they want to resolve to another chord (A major in this case).
They work well in most pop styles and sound even better
on a 12-string guitar!

Asus4

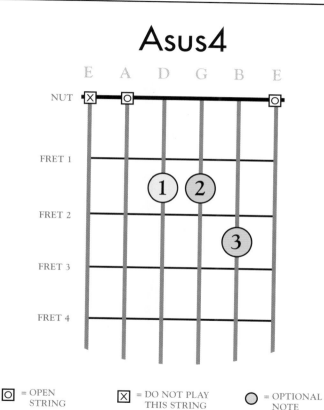

E A D G B E

NUT

FRET 1

① ②

FRET 2

③

FRET 3

FRET 4

⊡ = OPEN
STRING

☒ = DO NOT PLAY
THIS STRING

◯ = OPTIONAL
NOTE

The index finger plays the D string, 2nd fret. The middle finger plays
the G string, 2nd fret, and the ring finger plays the B string, 3rd fret.
The A and top E strings are open.

33

Adim

This shape uses all four fingers but is actually pretty easy.
Diminished chords have a jazzy and slightly scary sound all
on their own. Try moving this shape up the neck against the
open A string without shivering...

Adim

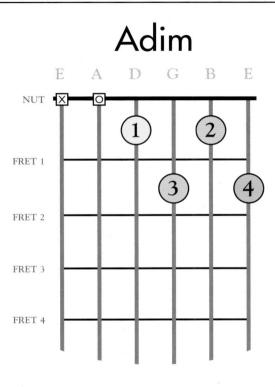

☐ = OPEN
STRING

☒ = DO NOT PLAY
THIS STRING

◯ = OPTIONAL
NOTE

The index finger plays the D string, 1st fret. The middle finger plays the B string, 1st fret. The ring finger plays the G string, 2nd fret, and the little finger plays the top E string, 3rd fret. The A string is open.

35

A6

Major sixth chords call to mind the swing era and also the final chord in many early Beatles songs. This one is very easy to play; adding the ring finger on the B string at the 4th fret changes it to a very sophisticated A6/9 chord.

A6

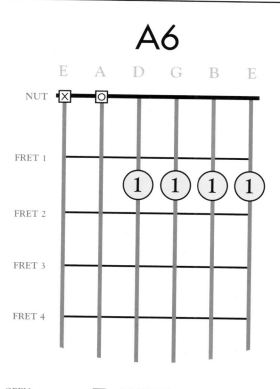

☐ = OPEN
   STRING

☒ = DO NOT PLAY
   THIS STRING

◯ = OPTIONAL
   NOTE

Use your index finger to play across the 2nd fret of the top E, B, G and
D strings.

37

A9

Many ninth shapes are a little tricky to play but this one is a bit easier and has a big, rich sound that is great for soul ballads or anything with a slightly jazzy feel.

A9

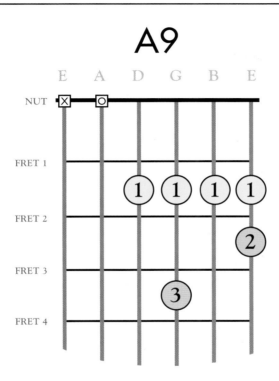

E   A   D   G   B   E

| ⊡ | = OPEN STRING | ☒ | = DO NOT PLAY THIS STRING | ◯ | = OPTIONAL NOTE |

Using your index finger, play across the 2nd fret of the top E, B, G and D strings, while your middle finger plays the 3rd fret of the top E string and your ring finger plays the 4th fret of the G string.

39

A barre

This is one of the most useful moveable barre shapes in any guitarist's repertoire. The E shape at the 5th fret gives us an A chord – a great alternative to the standard open shape. Try leaving the B and top E strings open instead of barring all the way – this produces a colourful alternative A(add9) shape.

A barre

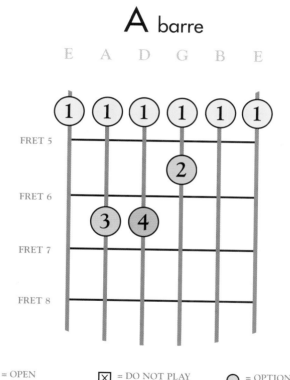

E A D G B E

FRET 5

FRET 6

FRET 7

FRET 8

⊙ = OPEN STRING   ☒ = DO NOT PLAY THIS STRING   ◯ = OPTIONAL NOTE

Make a barre across all six strings with your index finger at the 5th fret. The middle finger plays the G string, 6th fret; the ring and little fingers play the A and D strings respectively at the 7th fret.

41

B♭

This is the easiest shape for this chord. Try removing any of
the fretted notes and letting the open string sound (except
for the G string, which has the root note) for various rather
sophisticated sounds.

Bb

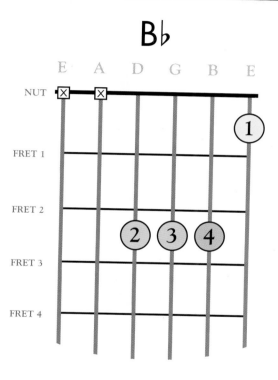

E	A	D	G	B	E

☒ = OPEN STRING   ☒ = DO NOT PLAY THIS STRING   ◯ = OPTIONAL NOTE

Let your index finger play the 1st fret of the top E string, your middle finger the 3rd fret of the D string and your ring finger the 3rd fret of the G string, then let your little finger play the 3rd fret of the B string.

43

B♭ (alt. shape)

This shape can be a little tricky but is well worth mastering.
Many players find it hard to get those three fingers in behind
the 3rd fret and make a half barre with the 3rd finger
instead. Extending this to the top E string produces a nice
Beatle-esque B♭6 chord.

Bb (alt. shape)

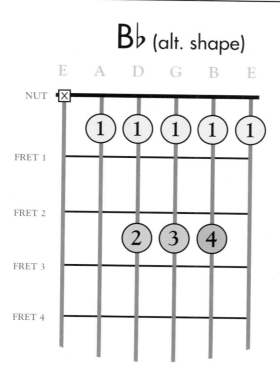

☐ = OPEN STRING

☒ = DO NOT PLAY THIS STRING

◯ = OPTIONAL NOTE

Using your index finger, play the 1st frets of the E, B, G, D and A strings, while your middle finger plays the 3rd fret of the D string, ring finger the 3rd fret of the G string and your little finger the 3rd fret of the B string.

B♭(add9)

Unfortunately there's no easy way to play this classic pop chord in this key, so this shape is quite a stretch. Many useful variations are possible: bring the little finger down two frets for a standard B♭ chord or remove it altogether for an alternative B♭7.

Bb (add9)

E A D G B E

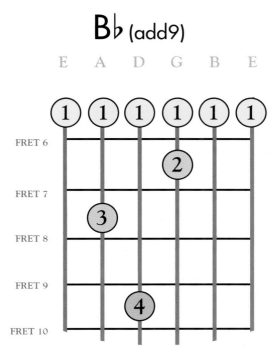

FRET 6

FRET 7

FRET 8

FRET 9

FRET 10

| | = OPEN STRING

| X | = DO NOT PLAY THIS STRING

◯ = OPTIONAL NOTE

Make a barre with your index finger across all six strings at the 6th fret.
Add the middle finger on the G string, 7th fret, the ring finger on the
A string, 8th fret, and the little finger on the D string, 10th fret.

B♭7

This is a fairly easy barre chord and useful for playing the blues in B♭ – very common in jazz. The other chords in a basic B♭ blues are E♭7 and F7.

Bb7

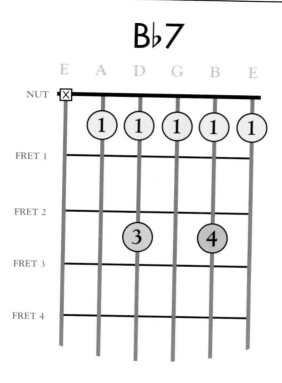

☐ = OPEN STRING

☒ = DO NOT PLAY THIS STRING

◯ = OPTIONAL NOTE

Use your index finger to play across the 1st frets of the top E, B, G, D and A strings, then your ring finger to play the 3rd fret of the D string and your little finger to play the 3rd fret of the B string.

B♭ MAJOR 7

This shape is well worth learning as it is fully moveable and
has a sweet, jazzy sound that is also great for soul, funk and
disco. Leaving the A string open produces a highly
mysterious sound that is too complex to name!

Bb MAJOR 7

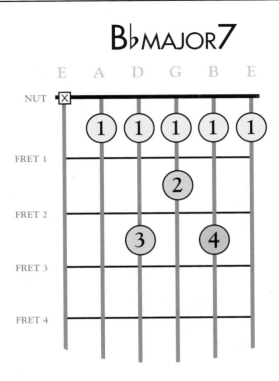

E   A   D   G   B   E

NUT

FRET 1

FRET 2

FRET 3

FRET 4

⊡ = OPEN STRING   ☒ = DO NOT PLAY THIS STRING   ◯ = OPTIONAL NOTE

Your index finger covers the 1st frets of the E, B, G, D and A strings.
Your middle finger plays the 2nd fret of the G string, your ring finger
the 3rd fret of the D string, your little finger the 3rd fret of the B string.

51

B♭m

This is a standard Em shape at the sixth fret. Barre chords
get easier as you move up the neck and the frets get closer
together. Be careful to barre all six strings, as open E or B
strings will sound very dissonant in this key.

Bbm

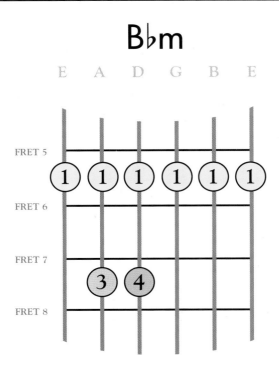

E   A   D   G   B   E

FRET 5

① ① ① ① ① ①

FRET 6

FRET 7

③ ④

FRET 8

▣ = OPEN STRING	☒ = DO NOT PLAY THIS STRING	⬤ = OPTIONAL NOTE

Let your index finger play across all six strings of the 6th fret, while your ring finger plays the 8th fret of the A string and your little finger plays the 8th fret of the D string.

B♭m (alt. shape)

Minor chords have a slightly sad sound; some listeners find the key of B♭ minor particularly dark. Try decorating this chord with a middle finger hammer-on, or even the middle, ring and little fingers together – great for funky/disco rhythm playing.

Bbm (alt. shape)

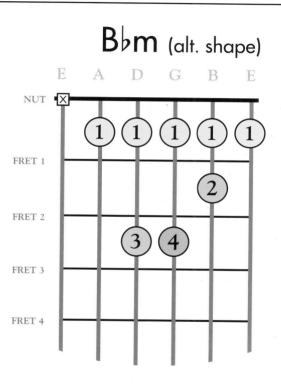

E A D G B E

NUT

FRET 1

FRET 2

FRET 3

FRET 4

☐ = OPEN STRING   ☒ = DO NOT PLAY THIS STRING   ◯ = OPTIONAL NOTE

Your index finger plays the E, B, G, D and A strings of the 1st fret,
your middle finger the 2nd fret of the B string, your ring finger the
3rd fret of the D string and your little finger the 3rd fret of the G string.

B♭m(add9)

This dark, gothic chord is quite a stretch. Try arpeggiating the notes; effects such as chorus or flanging can deepen the sense of mystery still further.

B♭m(add9)

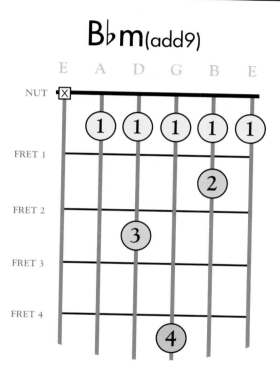

☐ = OPEN STRING	☒ = DO NOT PLAY THIS STRING
○ = OPTIONAL NOTE	

he index finger makes a barre across the A, D, G, B and top E strings at
e 1st fret. The middle finger plays the B string, 2nd fret. The ring finger
ays the D string, 3rd fret, and the little finger plays the G string, 5th fret.

57

B♭m7

Minor seventh chords are slightly jazzy and often sound as though they want to lead up a fourth to a dominant seventh chord – in this case E♭7. Try hammering on with the middle finger to decorate this chord.

B♭m7

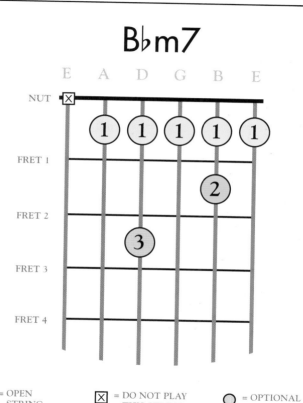

E · A · D · G · B · E

☐ = OPEN STRING ☒ = DO NOT PLAY THIS STRING ⬤ = OPTIONAL NOTE

Using your index finger, play the 1st fret of the top E, B, G, D and A strings, while your middle finger plays the 2nd fret of the B string and your ring finger the 3rd fret of the D string.

59

B♭sus4

This chord is great for all sorts of jangly pop. The suspension can be resolved by simply moving the little finger down to the 3rd fret, or of course it can be maintained indefinitely.

Bbsus4

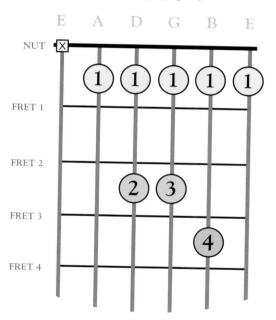

⬜ = OPEN STRING

❌ = DO NOT PLAY THIS STRING

⬤ = OPTIONAL NOTE

The index finger makes a barre across the A, D, G, B and top E strings at the 1st fret. The middle finger plays the D string, 3rd fret, the ring finger plays the G string, 3rd fret, and the little finger plays the B string, 4th fret.

B♭dim

This chord is actually moveable to some extent, even though it contains open strings, as diminished chords effectively repeat themselves every three frets. The positions in between will generally sound rather dissonant, as the open strings will clash with the chord.

Bbdim

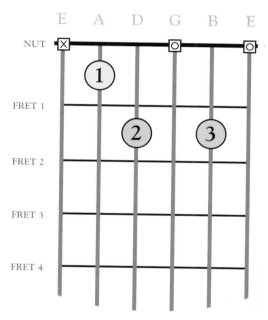

☐ = OPEN STRING	☒ = DO NOT PLAY THIS STRING
⬤ = OPTIONAL NOTE	

The index finger plays the A string, 1st fret. The middle finger plays the D string, 2nd fret, and the ring finger plays the B string, 2nd fret. The G and top E strings are open.

63

This is a fully moveable chord based on the A shape.
Getting those three fingers in at the same fret gets harder as
you move up the fretboard – one popular alternative is to
barre them all with the ring finger.

B

E	A	D	G	B	E

NUT

FRET 1

FRET 2

FRET 3

FRET 4

☐	= OPEN STRING	☒	= DO NOT PLAY THIS STRING	⬤	= OPTIONAL NOTE

t your index finger play the 2nd fret of the E, B, G, D and A strings.
ur middle finger plays the 4th fret of the D string, your ring finger the
h fret of the G string and your little finger the 4th fret of the B string.

B (alt. shape)

This is a useful shape, especially when playing with another guitarist. Try leaving the top E string open for a complex, poppy sound: B(add11).

B (alt. shape)

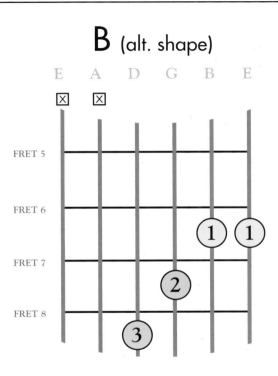

| E | A | D | G | B | E |

FRET 5

FRET 6

FRET 7

FRET 8

| ☐ = OPEN STRING | ☒ = DO NOT PLAY THIS STRING | ◯ = OPTIONAL NOTE |

ʝur index finger should play the 7th fret of both the top E and B strings,
ɦile your middle finger plays the 8th fret of the G string and your ring
ɪger plays the 9th fret of the D string.

B(add9)

This shape gets a little easier as you move up the fretboard
but is still rather tricky at the 2nd fret. Some players prefer
to play both the notes at the 4th fret with a half barre.

B(add9)

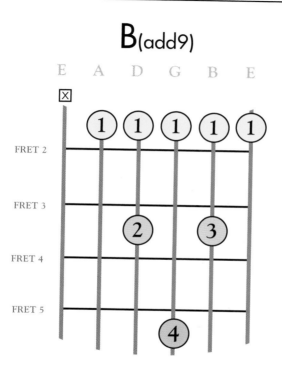

☐ = OPEN
STRING

☒ = DO NOT PLAY
THIS STRING

◯ = OPTIONAL
NOTE

he index finger makes a barre across the A, D, G, B and top E strings at
e 2nd fret. The middle finger plays the D string, 4th fret. The ring finger
ays the B string, 4th fret and the little finger plays the G string, 6th fret.

B7

Many players learn this chord fairly early in order to play songs in E or E minor, and it sounds great whether strummed or picked. Try raising the little finger to the 3rd fret for a more complex sound (B7#5) before resolving back to B7.

B7

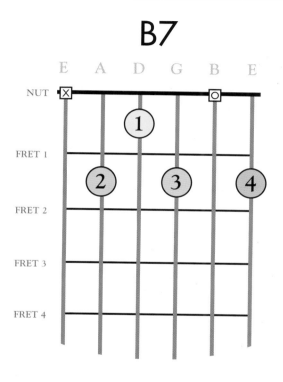

☐ = OPEN STRING

☒ = DO NOT PLAY THIS STRING

◯ = OPTIONAL NOTE

Your index finger should play the 1st fret of the D string, your middle finger the 2nd fret of the A string, your ring finger the 2nd fret of the G string and your little finger the 2nd fret of the top E.

BMAJOR7

This moveable shape produces a Bmaj7 at the 2nd fret –
highly useful for a soul or jazz feel in the key of B or F#.
Removing the middle finger results in a useful
alternative B7 shape.

BMAJOR7

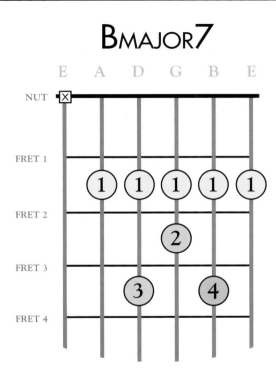

E   A   D   G   B   E

NUT

FRET 1

FRET 2

FRET 3

FRET 4

| ◯ = OPEN STRING | ☒ = DO NOT PLAY THIS STRING | ◯ = OPTIONAL NOTE |

over the 2nd frets of the E, B, G, D and A strings with your index finger.
our middle finger plays the 3rd fret of the G string, your ring finger the
th fret of the D string and your little finger the 4th fret of the B string.

Bm

This is the moveable Em shape at the 7th fret – a very useful chord for many styles. Harmonics are easily produced at the 7th fret – after playing this chord, try placing the index finger very lightly across the top three strings, exactly above the fret, and strum. This never fails to impress non-guitarists.

Bm

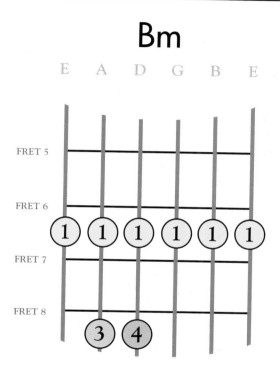

E   A   D   G   B   E

☐ = OPEN STRING

☒ = DO NOT PLAY THIS STRING

◯ = OPTIONAL NOTE

sing your index finger play across all six strings of the 7th fret,
hile letting your ring finger play the 9th fret of the A string and
our little finger play the 9th fret of the D string.

Bm (alt. shape)

This version of B minor is barred at the 2nd fret.
All sorts of effects and embellishments are possible here –
try changing this into a 'lazy' barre chord by incorporating
the open top E string, resulting in a complex-sounding but
easy Bm(add11) chord.

Bm (alt. shape)

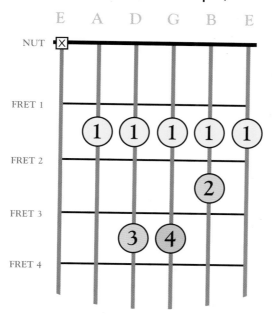

☐ = OPEN STRING   ☒ = DO NOT PLAY THIS STRING   ◯ = OPTIONAL NOTE

et your index finger play the 2nd fret of the E, B, G, D and A strings,
our middle finger the 3rd fret of the B string, your ring finger the 4th
et of the D string and your little finger the 4th fret of the G string.

77

Bm(add9)

This shape is quite a stretch at the 2nd fret. For an even
richer sounding (but slightly easier) shape, try letting the top
E string remain open (don't make the barre).

Bm(add9)

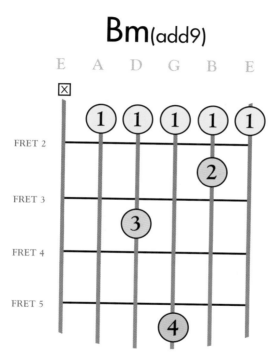

E   A   D   G   B   E

FRET 2

FRET 3

FRET 4

FRET 5

☐ = OPEN STRING

☒ = DO NOT PLAY THIS STRING

◯ = OPTIONAL NOTE

The index finger makes a barre across the A, D, G, B and top E strings at the 2nd fret. The middle finger plays the B string, 3rd fret. The ring finger plays the D string, 4th fret, and the little finger plays the G string, 6th fret.

79

Bm7

This shape is based on the B7 shape – simply remove the
index finger to let the open D string sound. This chord has a
slightly folky sound when finger-picked; any of the fretted
notes can be hammered on for interesting effects.

Bm7

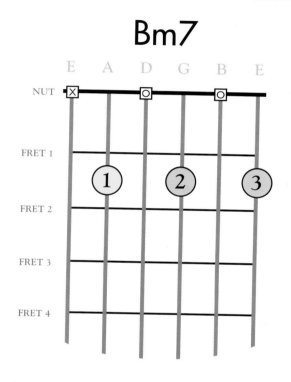

E A D G B E

NUT

FRET 1

FRET 2

FRET 3

FRET 4

1   2   3

◯ = OPEN STRING   ☒ = DO NOT PLAY THIS STRING   ◯ = OPTIONAL NOTE

ur index finger should play the 2nd fret of the A string, while your
ddle finger plays the 2nd fret of the G string and your ring finger the
d fret of the top E string.

Bsus4

This jangly pop chord is very useful for songs in B major,
E major and E minor. Removing the little finger produces
a different but equally interesting suspension – Bsus2.

Bsus4

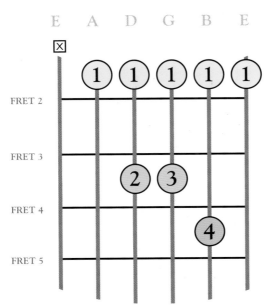

E   A   D   G   B   E

☐ = OPEN STRING   ☒ = DO NOT PLAY THIS STRING   ◯ = OPTIONAL NOTE

e index finger makes a barre across the A, D, G, B and top E strings at e 2nd fret. The middle finger plays the D string, 4th fret. The ring finger ays the G string, 4th fret, and the little finger plays the B string, 5th fret.

Bdim

This diminished shape is fully moveable – just make sure you don't let the unplayed strings sound ... unless you want to, of course, but be prepared for some rather dissonant sounds.

Bdim

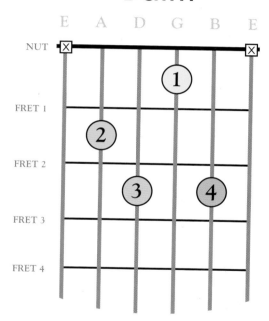

E A D G B E

NUT

FRET 1

FRET 2

FRET 3

FRET 4

⊡ = OPEN STRING

☒ = DO NOT PLAY THIS STRING

◯ = OPTIONAL NOTE

he index finger plays the G string, 1st fret. The middle finger plays the
string, 2nd fret. The ring finger plays the D string, 3rd fret, and the little
ger plays the B string, 3rd fret.

85

B6

Holding these two barres down at once can be a little tricky but the result is a fully moveable and very colourful chord – particularly good as a final chord if you want to add a hint of '60s flavour.

B6

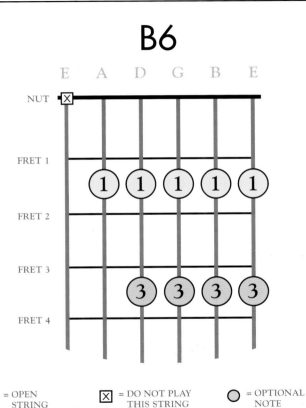

E   A   D   G   B   E

NUT

FRET 1

FRET 2

FRET 3

FRET 4

⊡ = OPEN STRING   ⊠ = DO NOT PLAY THIS STRING   ◯ = OPTIONAL NOTE

he index finger makes a barre across the A, D, G, B and top E strings
 the 2nd fret. The ring finger makes a barre across the D, G, B and top
strings at the 4th fret.

B9

This ninth shape is great for funk and disco rhythm playing –
it's impossible to play without thinking of James Brown.
As there are no open strings, the chord is moveable –
try playing the chord and then sliding up one fret for
a classic funk effect.

B9

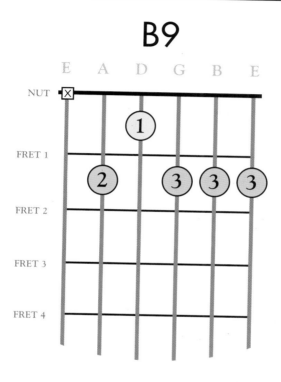

E A D G B E

NUT

FRET 1

FRET 2

FRET 3

FRET 4

| ☐ | = OPEN STRING | ☒ | = DO NOT PLAY THIS STRING | ◯ | = OPTIONAL NOTE |

he index finger plays the D string, 1st fret. The middle finger plays the
string, 2nd fret, and the ring finger makes a barre across the G, B and
p E strings at the 2nd fret.

B barre

This is a fully moveable barre chord based on the E shape.
Try leaving the B and top E strings open: this big complex
chord is called B(add11) and instantly conjures up the sound
of jangly indie guitar pop.

B barre

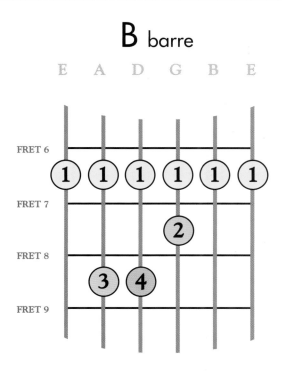

E   A   D   G   B   E

FRET 6

FRET 7

FRET 8

FRET 9

◻ = OPEN STRING   ☒ = DO NOT PLAY THIS STRING   ◯ = OPTIONAL NOTE

he index finger makes a barre across all six strings at the 7th fret.
he middle finger plays the G string, 8th fret. The ring finger plays the
string, 9th fret, and the little finger plays the D string, 9th fret.

C

This shape is relatively easy to learn for many three-chord songs in C, F and G. Try adding the little finger on the B string, 3rd fret, for a great-sounding and easy alternative shape for C(add9).

C

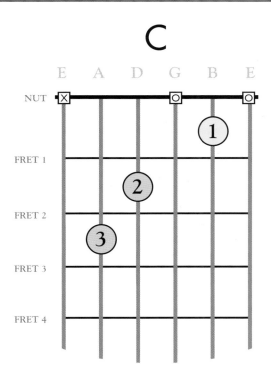

☐ = OPEN STRING ☒ = DO NOT PLAY THIS STRING ◯ = OPTIONAL NOTE

ur index finger should play the 1st fret of the B string, while your
iddle finger plays the 2nd fret of the D string and your ring finger
e 3rd fret of the A string.

C (alt. shape)

This is a strong alternative to the basic C shape. An even more 'ringy' version can be produced by not making the barre, but rather letting the open top E string sound to produce a unison at the top of the chord.

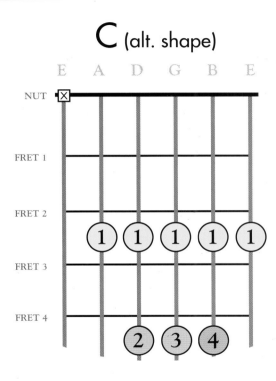

C (alt. shape)

E   A   D   G   B   E

NUT

FRET 1

FRET 2

FRET 3

FRET 4

| ☐ = OPEN STRING | ☒ = DO NOT PLAY THIS STRING | ◯ = OPTIONAL NOTE |

...t your index finger play the 3rd frets of the E, B, G, D and A strings,
...ur middle finger the 5th fret of the D string, your ring finger the
...h fret of the G string and your little finger the 5th fret of the B string.

C(add9)

This shape is still a bit of a stretch at the third fret but it's worth some perseverance. This shape can be viewed as the 'pop' version.

C(add9)

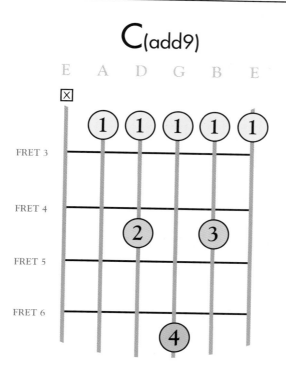

E   A   D   G   B   E

FRET 3

FRET 4

FRET 5

FRET 6

| ☐ | = OPEN STRING | ☒ | = DO NOT PLAY THIS STRING | ◯ | = OPTIONAL NOTE |

he index finger makes a barre across the A, D, G, B and top E strings at
e 3rd fret. The middle finger plays the D string, 5th fret. The ring finger
ays the B string, 5th fret, and the little finger plays the G string, 7th fret.

C7

This seventh chord has a big, rich sound. C7 is used in the
12-bar blues sequence in C, F or G. Try moving the fretted
notes up two frets against the open top E string for
an alternative D9 shape.

C7

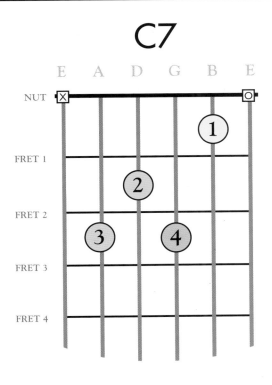

| ☐ | = OPEN STRING | ☒ | = DO NOT PLAY THIS STRING | ◯ | = OPTIONAL NOTE |

se your index finger to play the 1st fret of the B string, your middle
nger the 2nd fret of the D string, your ring finger the 3rd fret of the
string and your little finger the 3rd fret of the G string.

CMAJOR7

This is a very easy shape and great for songs in C or G with a
jazzy flavour. Major seventh shapes often sound good with
chorus or phasing; try adding the little finger on the top E
string, 3rd fret, for an alternative voicing.

Cmajor7

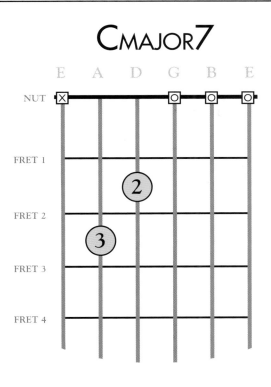

E	A	D	G	B	E

```
O = OPEN          X = DO NOT PLAY       O = OPTIONAL
    STRING            THIS STRING           NOTE
```

To play this chord you can use either your index and middle fingers
or your ring and little fingers – use whichever combination feels best.
Play the 2nd fret of the D string and the 3rd fret of the A string.

Cm

This basic Cm shape can be embellished by hammering on with the middle, ring or little finger – or even all of them. Removing all of them and allowing just the barred notes to sound produces a rich C11 chord.

Cm

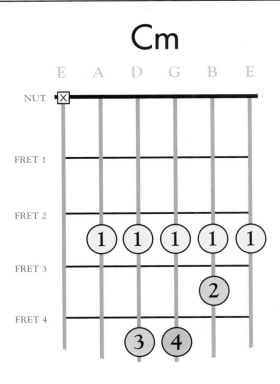

E   A   D   G   B   E

NUT

FRET 1

FRET 2

FRET 3

FRET 4

⊡ = OPEN
STRING

☒ = DO NOT PLAY
THIS STRING

◯ = OPTIONAL
NOTE

Your index finger plays the 3rd fret of the E, B, G, D and A strings, your middle finger the 4th fret of the B string, your ring finger the 5th fret of the D string and your little finger the 5th fret of the G string.

103

Cm (alt. shape)

The Cm chord goes well with Fm and Gm in the key of C minor, or Fm and B♭m in the key of F minor. Removing the little finger produces an alternative Cm7 shape; moving it to the top E string, 10th fret, results in a jazzy Cm9.

Cm (alt. shape)

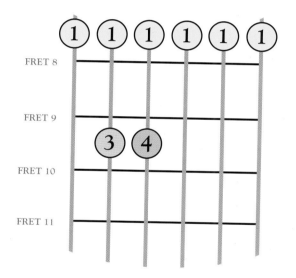

E   A   D   G   B   E

FRET 8

FRET 9

FRET 10

FRET 11

☐ = OPEN STRING   ☒ = DO NOT PLAY THIS STRING   ◯ = OPTIONAL NOTE

ing your index finger play across the 8th fret of all the strings, while
ur ring finger plays the 10th fret of the A string and your little finger
ys the 10th fret of the D string.

Cm(add9)

This soulful, moody chord sounds both poppy and folky at the same time. The shape is a little easier at this fret but still a bit of a stretch – moving the little finger down two frets for a standard Cm is always an option when it starts to ache!

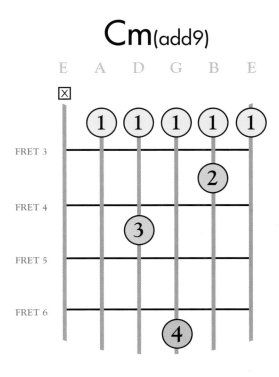

Cm(add9)

| = OPEN STRING | | = DO NOT PLAY THIS STRING | | = OPTIONAL NOTE |

e index finger makes a barre across the A, D, G, B and top E strings at
3rd fret. The middle finger plays the B string, 4th fret. The ring finger
ys the D string, 5th fret, and the little finger plays the G string, 7th fret.

107

Cm7

This Cm shape is a fairly easy barre chord with a jazzy flavour. Adding the little finger on the top E string, 6th fret, gives it a richer sound; moving it down a fret to the 5th fret results in a plangent Cm13 chord.

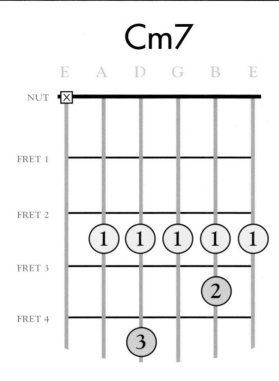

Cm7

| E | A | D | G | B | E |

NUT ☒

FRET 1

FRET 2

① ① ① ① ①

FRET 3

②

FRET 4

③

○ = OPEN STRING   ☒ = DO NOT PLAY THIS STRING   ◯ = OPTIONAL NOTE

r index finger should cover the 3rd fret of the top E, B, G, D and A
ngs, while your middle finger plays the 4th fret of the B string and
r ring finger the 5th fret of the D string.

Csus4

Suspended chords are used in pop, folk and country music.
This shape can be turned into something rather unusual by
letting the top E string sound open rather than making the
barre – a quirky sounding C(add11) chord.

Csus4

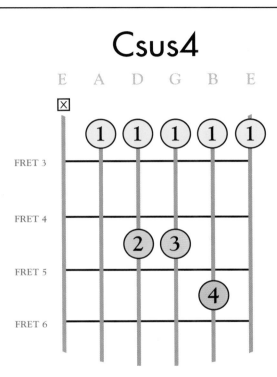

E   A   D   G   B   E

FRET 3

FRET 4

FRET 5

FRET 6

| ☐ | = OPEN STRING | ☒ | = DO NOT PLAY THIS STRING | ⬤ | = OPTIONAL NOTE |

he index finger makes a barre across the A, D, G, B and top E strings at
e 3rd fret. The middle finger plays the D string, 5th fret. The ring finger
ays the G string, 5th fret, and the little finger plays the B string, 6th fret.

Cdim

Diminished chords can stand in for many other chords.
You may not know how to play a 7b9 chord but you can use
a diminished shape instead. Cdim can be substituted for
B7♭9, D7♭9, F7♭9 or A♭7♭9.

Cdim

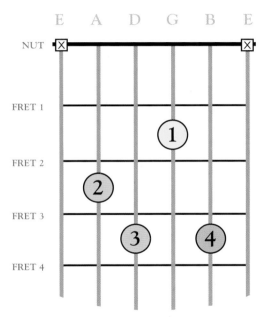

☐ = OPEN STRING   ☒ = DO NOT PLAY THIS STRING   ◯ = OPTIONAL NOTE

he index finger plays the G string, 2nd fret. The middle finger plays the
string, 3rd fret. The ring finger plays the D string, 4th fret, and the little
ger plays the B string, 4th fret.

113

C6

This shape is formed by adding the little finger to the
standard Am shape. In fact, these two chords share the same
set of notes, but take different root notes. This shape sounds
great for swing/jazz strumming, and produces a colourful
D6/9 chord if the fretted notes are moved up by two frets
against the open top E string.

C6

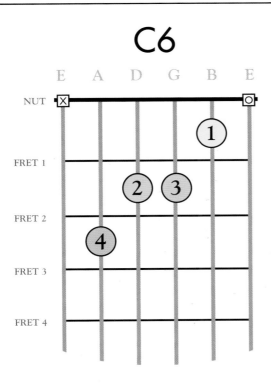

E   A   D   G   B   E

NUT

FRET 1

FRET 2

FRET 3

FRET 4

⊙ = OPEN STRING   ⊠ = DO NOT PLAY THIS STRING   ◯ = OPTIONAL NOTE

ing your index finger, play the 1st fret of the B string, while your
ddle finger plays the 2nd fret of the D string, your ring finger the
d fret of the G string and your little finger the 3rd fret of the A string.

C9

This version of the C9 shape sounds rather jazzy; the interval between the top two strings adds a hint of sophistication. For the funkier version, the ring finger is barred across the top three strings at the 3rd fret.

C9

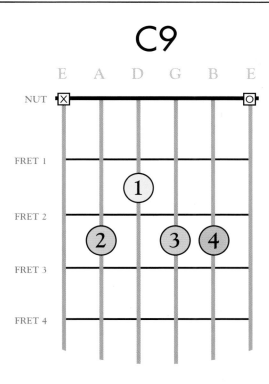

E   A   D   G   B   E

NUT

FRET 1

FRET 2

FRET 3

FRET 4

◯ = OPEN STRING   ☒ = DO NOT PLAY THIS STRING   ⬤ = OPTIONAL NOTE

Your index finger should play the 2nd fret of the D string, your middle finger the 3rd fret of the A string, your ring finger the 3rd fret of the G string and your little finger the 3rd fret of the B string.

C#

This moveable barre shape based on the C chord can take a bit of mastering but the result is worth it, giving a C# or D♭ major at the 1st fret. Many players make the barre all the way to the A string; the little finger can then simply be removed to give a B♭m7 chord.

C#

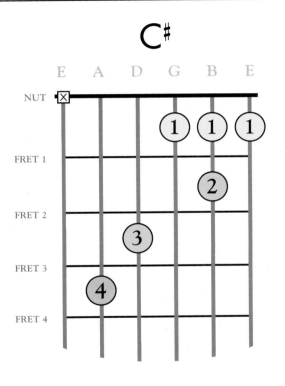

E	A	D	G	B	E

☐ = OPEN STRING

☒ = DO NOT PLAY THIS STRING

⬤ = OPTIONAL NOTE

et your index finger cover the 1st frets of the E, B and G strings. Your
iiddle finger plays the 2nd fret of the B string, your ring finger the
:rd fret of the D string and your little finger the 4th fret of the A string.

C# (alt. shape)

The A shape barred at the 4th fret produces a C# major
chord. This is one position where the 'lazy barre'
effect (letting the top string sound open instead of making
the barre) is not usually a good idea, as the result will be
rather dissonant.

C# (alt. shape)

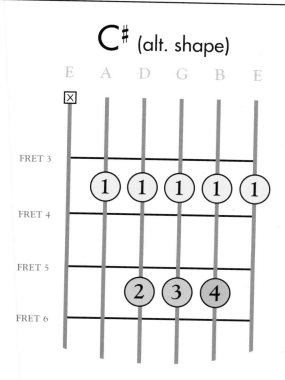

☒ = DO NOT PLAY THIS STRING   ◯ = OPTIONAL NOTE   ⊙ = OPEN STRING

your index finger cover the 4th frets of the E, B, G, D and A strings.
ur middle finger plays the 6th fret of the D string, your ring finger the
fret of the G string and your little finger the 6th fret of the B string.

C#(add9)

This shape should be getting easier as you move
up the fretboard but may still be a bit of a stretch.
One alternative is to barre the E(add9) shape at the
9th fret – see B♭(add9) on p46.

C#(add9)

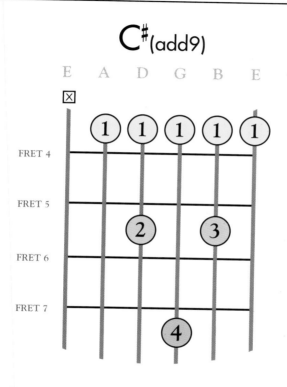

☒ = OPEN STRING   ☒ = DO NOT PLAY THIS STRING   ◯ = OPTIONAL NOTE

e index finger makes a barre across the A, D, G, B and top E strings at
4th fret. The middle finger plays the D string, 6th fret. The ring finger
ys the B string, 6th fret, and the little finger plays the G string, 8th fret.

123

C#7

Dominant seventh chords are found in most pop styles, particularly blues and jazz. C#7 can be used to spice up a bluesy chord sequence in E. In this key, C#7 resolves to F#m7, which leads on to B7 and back to E.

C#7

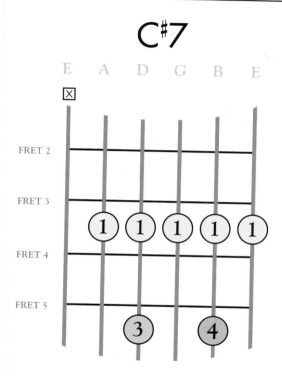

E   A   D   G   B   E

FRET 2

FRET 3

FRET 4

FRET 5

☐ = OPEN STRING

☒ = DO NOT PLAY THIS STRING

○ = OPTIONAL NOTE

e your index finger to play across the 4th fret of the E, B, G, D and A ings, then use your ring finger to play the 6th fret of the D string and ur little finger to play the 6th fret of the B string.

C#MAJOR7

This chord sounds really cool when substituted for a final F chord in the key of F major, though the correct name for the chord in this context is actually D♭maj7. This can resolve to an F chord; you can delay the resolution still further by inserting a G♭maj7.

C#MAJOR7

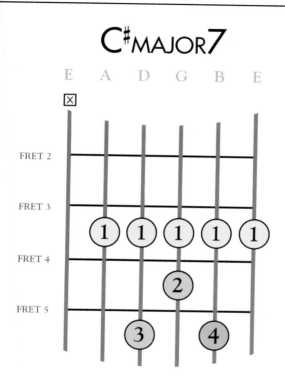

E   A   D   G   B   E

FRET 2

FRET 3

FRET 4

FRET 5

☒ = OPEN
STRING

☒ = DO NOT PLAY
THIS STRING

◯ = OPTIONAL
NOTE

t your index finger play the 4th fret of the E, B, G, D and A strings. Your
ddle finger plays the 5th fret of the G string, your ring finger the 6th
t of the D string and your little finger the 6th fret of the B string.

127

C[#]m

The 'lazy' barre trick works well with this chord – leaving the top E string open puts a unison at the top of the chord for a thick, 'ringy' sound. Leaving the B string open too produces an interesting alternative C#m7 shape.

C#m

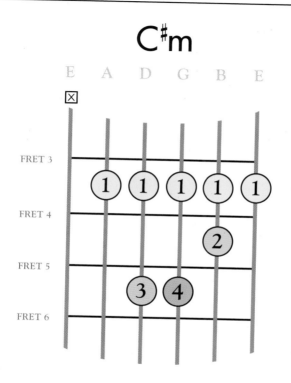

E A D G B E

FRET 3

FRET 4

FRET 5

FRET 6

☐ = OPEN STRING   ☒ = DO NOT PLAY THIS STRING   ○ = OPTIONAL NOTE

t your index finger play the 4th fret of the top E, B, G, D and A strings,
ur middle finger the 5th fret of the B string, your ring finger the 6th fret
the D string and your little finger the 6th fret of the G string.

129

C#m (alt. shape)

This version of the C#m chord is very versatile; when moving to F#m, as many songs do, try joining the chords up by letting the open bottom E string sound against the rest of the C#m shape for one or two beats before the change.

C#m (alt. shape)

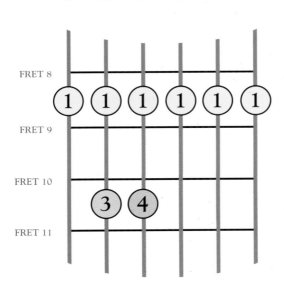

E   A   D   G   B   E

FRET 8

FRET 9

FRET 10

FRET 11

| ☐ = OPEN STRING | ☒ = DO NOT PLAY THIS STRING | ◯ = OPTIONAL NOTE |

ing your index finger play across the 9th fret of all the strings, while
ur ring finger plays the 11th fret of the A string and your little finger
ays the 11th fret of the D string.

C#m(add9)

This chord is very useful in the key of E and works well with other 'add9' chords. Try stringing together E(add9), C#m(add9), A(add9) and B(add9) and you'll find yourself writing a song in no time – but be careful: it's been done before!

C#m(add9)

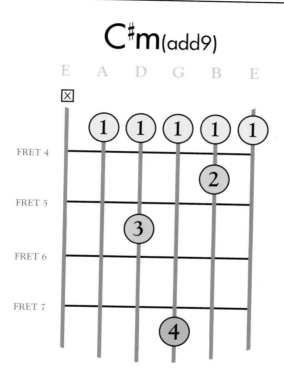

FRET 4

FRET 5

FRET 6

FRET 7

☐ = OPEN
STRING

☒ = DO NOT PLAY
THIS STRING

◯ = OPTIONAL
NOTE

he index finger makes a barre across the A, D, G, B and top E strings at
e 4th fret. The middle finger plays the B string, 5th fret. The ring finger
ays the D string, 6th fret, and the little finger plays the G string, 8th fret.

C#m7

Most barre chords, including this one, can also be
played as power chords by simply playing only the two
lowest fretted notes. Try playing the power chord in a steady
pulse, adding the full chord every so often for variety.

C#m7

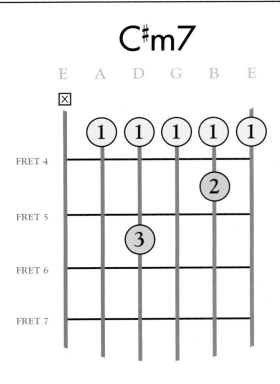

E   A   D   G   B   E

FRET 4

FRET 5

FRET 6

FRET 7

◻ = OPEN STRING   ⊠ = DO NOT PLAY THIS STRING   ◯ = OPTIONAL NOTE

et your index finger cover the 4th fret of the top E, B, G, D and A strings,
hile your middle finger plays the 5th fret of the B string and your ring
nger the 6th fret of the D string.

C#sus4

Suspensions can be created and released repeatedly.
This one resolves to C# major by moving the little finger
down to the 6th fret. Try repeating this rhythmically
(perhaps a bar of each) before resolving to F# or F#m.

C#sus4

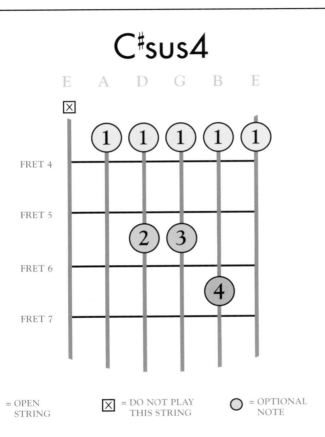

E   A   D   G   B   E

FRET 4

FRET 5

FRET 6

FRET 7

◯ = OPEN
STRING

☒ = DO NOT PLAY
THIS STRING

◯ = OPTIONAL
NOTE

e index finger makes a barre across the A, D, G, B and top E strings at
4th fret. The middle finger plays the D string, 6th fret. The ring finger
ys the G string, 6th fret, and the little finger plays the B string, 7th fret.

137

C#dim

The open top E string can be added to this shape to give a resonant unison at the top of the chord. Try picking the chord, moving the shape three frets up the neck and picking before moving up a further three frets.

C#dim

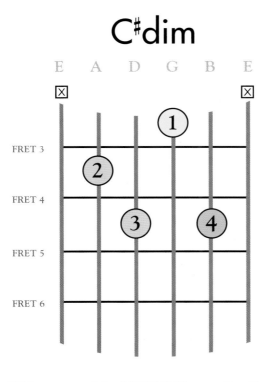

| = OPEN STRING | ☒ = DO NOT PLAY THIS STRING | ◯ = OPTIONAL NOTE |

index finger plays the G string, 3rd fret. The middle finger plays the string, 4th fret. The ring finger plays the D string, 5th fret, and the little er plays the B string, 5th fret.

139

D

The D chord is one of the first chords many players learn
and lends itself to the sort of tricks many folk/country
players use: add the little finger on the top string, 3rd fret
for Dsus4, remove it again, remove the middle finger for
Dsus2, repeat forever...

D

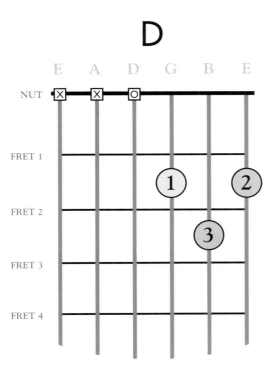

E A D G B E

NUT

FRET 1

① ②

FRET 2

③

FRET 3

FRET 4

⊙ = OPEN STRING

☒ = DO NOT PLAY THIS STRING

◯ = OPTIONAL NOTE

r index finger should play the 2nd fret of the G string, while your
dle finger plays the 2nd fret of the top E and your ring finger plays
3rd fret of the B string.

D (alt. shape)

This shape can be varied in many interesting ways:
let the top E string sound open for an alternative D(add9)
shape; adding the open B string produces a
clever-sounding D6/9.

D (alt. shape)

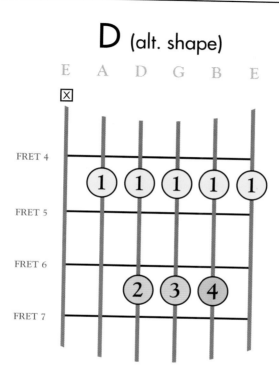

| O | = OPEN STRING | | X | = DO NOT PLAY THIS STRING | | ◯ | = OPTIONAL NOTE |

e index finger makes a barre across the A, D, G, B and top E strings at
5th fret. The middle, ring and little fingers play the D, G and B strings
pectively at the 7th fret.

143

D(add9)

This shape is a bit of a handful but is well worth mastering as the voicing can make it sound more like piano than guitar! The tricky part is preventing the index finger from touching the top E string; giving up and letting it form a barre across the top three strings results in a handy moveable alternative D shape.

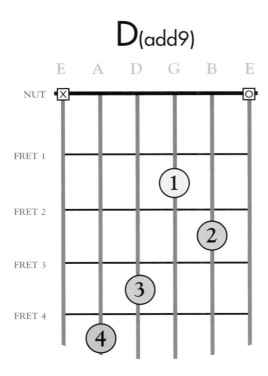

D(add9)

E   A   D   G   B   E

NUT

FRET 1

FRET 2

FRET 3

FRET 4

| ◯ | = OPEN STRING | ☒ | = DO NOT PLAY THIS STRING | ◯ | = OPTIONAL NOTE |

e index finger plays the G string, 2nd fret. The middle finger plays the
tring, 3rd fret. The ring finger plays the D string, 4th fret, and the little
ger plays the A string, 5th fret.

D7

This chord is useful as a colourful alternative to the D chord when playing in the key of G. Adding the little finger on the top string, 3rd fret, results in a D7sus4 chord.

D7

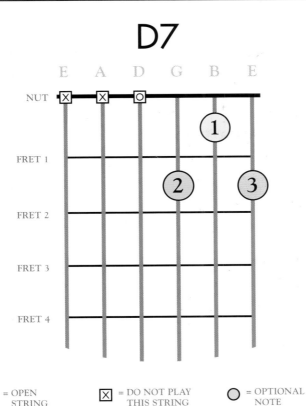

| E | A | D | G | B | E |

NUT

FRET 1

FRET 2

FRET 3

FRET 4

⊡ = OPEN STRING   ☒ = DO NOT PLAY THIS STRING   ◯ = OPTIONAL NOTE

...et your index finger play the 1st fret of the B string, while your middle ...ger should play the 2nd fret of the G string and finally your ring finger ...ays the 2nd fret of the top E string.

DMAJOR7

This jazzy major seventh can be turned into an even more sophisticated sounding Dmaj9 by letting the top E string sound open. Either version sounds great whether picked or strummed.

Dmajor7

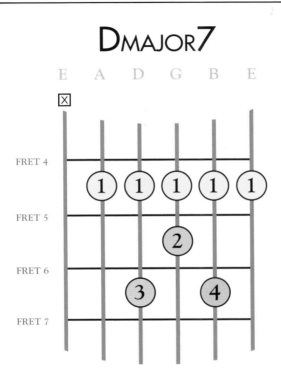

E   A   D   G   B   E

☐ = OPEN
STRING

☒ = DO NOT PLAY
THIS STRING

○ = OPTIONAL
NOTE

Let your index finger play the 5th fret of the E, B, G, D and A strings, your middle finger the 6th fret of the G string, your ring finger the 7th fret of the D string and your little finger the 7th fret of the B string.

Dm

D minor has been called 'the saddest of all keys' and this effect certainly comes across on the guitar. Dm is used in many folk songs in the key of A minor; playing around with the little finger at the 3rd fret on the top E string (Dsus4) brings the Rolling Stones' 'Paint It Black' to mind.

Dm

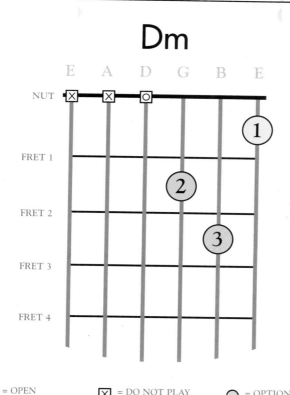

E	A	D	G	B	E

⊡ = OPEN STRING	☒ = DO NOT PLAY THIS STRING
◯ = OPTIONAL NOTE	

Let your index finger play the 1st fret of the top E string, while your middle finger plays the 2nd fret of the G string and your ring finger plays the 3rd fret of the B string.

Dm (alt. shape)

This Dm shape can be turned into an easier shape for
Dm(add9) by letting the top E string sound open.
Adding the open A string results in a sophisticated
classical second inversion.

Dm (alt. shape)

E A D G B E

FRET 5

FRET 6

FRET 7

FRET 8

◻ = OPEN STRING   ☒ = DO NOT PLAY THIS STRING   ◯ = OPTIONAL NOTE

t your index finger play the 5th fret of the E, B, G, D and A strings,
ur middle finger the 6th fret of the B string, your ring finger the 7th
t of the D string and your little finger the 7th fret of the G string.

153

Dm(add9)

The five-fret stretch in this shape isn't too bad at the
5th fret, especially on electric guitar.

Dm(add9)

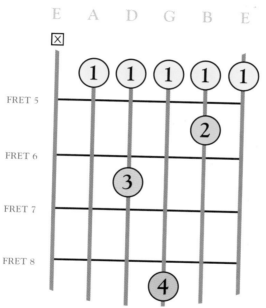

◯ = OPEN STRING   ☒ = DO NOT PLAY THIS STRING   ◯ = OPTIONAL NOTE

e index finger makes a barre across the A, D, G, B and top E strings at
5th fret. The middle finger plays the B string, 6th fret. The ring finger
ys the D string, 7th fret, and the little finger plays the G string, 9th fret.

155

Dm7

This is a very simple and effective chord shape.
In the key of C, this chord 'wants' to go to G7 and then C;
this can be delayed by adding the middle finger on the
low E string, 3rd fret, to produce a G11 chord.

Dm7

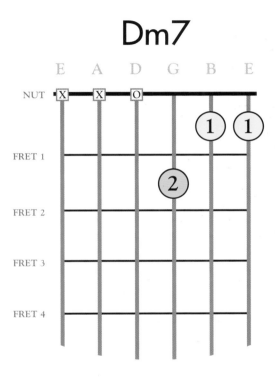

⊙ = OPEN STRING   ⊠ = DO NOT PLAY THIS STRING   ◯ = OPTIONAL NOTE

e index finger plays the first fret of both the B and top E strings.
e middle finger plays the G string, 2nd fret. The D string is open.

Dsus4

This chord is a favourite with folk guitarists everywhere.
Though not shown in chord boxes, the middle finger is
usually placed on the top E string at the 2nd fret so the little
finger can be lifted to produce a D chord.

Dsus4

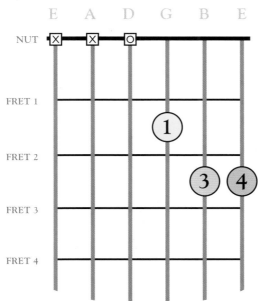

E   A   D   G   B   E

NUT

FRET 1

FRET 2

FRET 3

FRET 4

◯ = OPEN STRING   ☒ = DO NOT PLAY THIS STRING   ◯ = OPTIONAL NOTE

index finger plays the G string, 2nd fret. The ring finger plays the
ring, 3rd fret, and the little finger plays the top E string, 3rd fret.

159

Ddim

This complex-sounding diminished chord is actually easy to play, requiring only two fingers. Try playing it instead of an E7; if you like you can add the open bottom E string, making a full E7(♭9)

Ddim

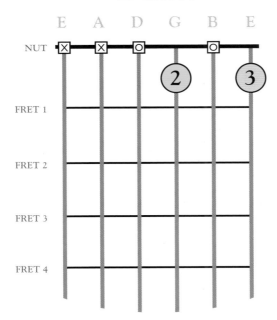

◯ = OPEN STRING

☒ = DO NOT PLAY THIS STRING

◯ = OPTIONAL NOTE

e middle finger plays the G string, 1st fret, and the ring finger plays
: top E string, 1st fret. The D and B strings are open.

D6

Moving the fretted notes of the D diminished chord up by
two frets produces this major sixth shape. Sliding between
the two sounds rather cool.

D6

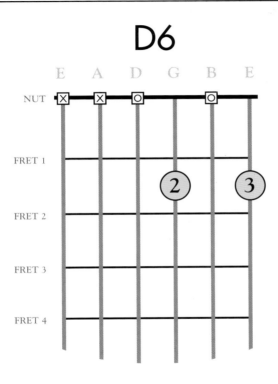

E A D G B E

NUT

FRET 1

FRET 2

FRET 3

FRET 4

| ⊡ = OPEN STRING | ⊠ = DO NOT PLAY THIS STRING | ◯ = OPTIONAL NOTE |

or this chord you can use either your index and middle fingers, or ur middle and ring fingers, to play the 2nd fret of the G string and e top E string.

D9

This easy shape sounds good but is actually not a proper D9 chord. For a full D9, try moving the fretted notes of C7 up by two frets, keeping the open top E string.

D9

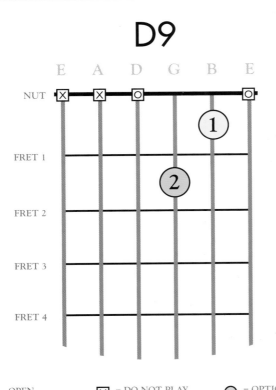

| | | | | | |
|E|A|D|G|B|E|

NUT

FRET 1

FRET 2

FRET 3

FRET 4

⃞O = OPEN STRING   ⌧ = DO NOT PLAY THIS STRING   ◯ = OPTIONAL NOTE

...is is an easy one! Let your index finger play the 1st fret of the B string
...d your middle finger play the 2nd fret of the G string. The D string and
...e top E string should be played open.

165

E♭

This strange shape is the only practical way to play E♭ in first position. Try moving the index finger to the bottom E string, 3rd fret, for a cool-sounding first inversion: E♭/G (or use your thumb for this).

E♭

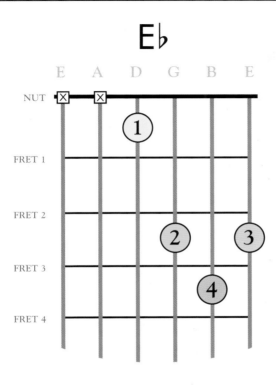

| E | A | D | G | B | E |

NUT

FRET 1

FRET 2

FRET 3

FRET 4

= OPEN STRING   = DO NOT PLAY THIS STRING   = OPTIONAL NOTE

ur index finger should play the 1st fret of the D string, your middle
ger the 3rd fret of the G string, your ring finger the 3rd fret of the
E string and your little finger the 4th fret of the B string.

E♭ (alt. shape)

This moveable shape is based on the C chord.
Extending the barre across all six strings produces a first
inversion which is great as a passing chord. Try using this
between Fm and A♭.

E♭ (alt. shape)

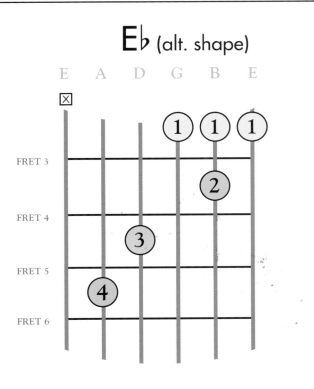

E   A   D   G   B   E

FRET 3

FRET 4

FRET 5

FRET 6

☐ = OPEN STRING   ☒ = DO NOT PLAY THIS STRING   ○ = OPTIONAL NOTE

Your index finger covers the 3rd fret of the E, B and G strings, while your middle finger plays the 4th fret of the B string, your ring finger the 5th fret of the D string and your little finger the 6th fret of the A string.

E♭ (add9)

The bottom three notes here are really the essential ones,
so you can get away with just these if the whole chord is too
much of a stretch. Try moving these three notes around the
fretboard randomly – this can sound rather unusual.

E♭ (add9)

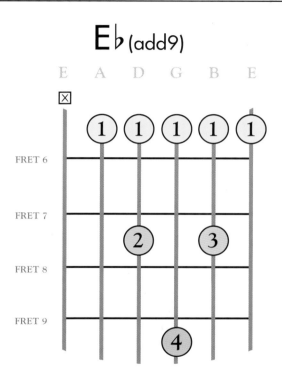

E   A   D   G   B   E

FRET 6

FRET 7

FRET 8

FRET 9

☐ = OPEN STRING   ☒ = DO NOT PLAY THIS STRING   ◯ = OPTIONAL NOTE

he index finger makes a barre across the A, D, G, B and top E strings at e 6th fret. The middle finger plays the D string, 8th fret, the ring finger e B string, 8th fret, and the little finger plays the G string, 10th fret.

E♭7

E♭7 is a vital chord in a B♭ blues, which you will probably be asked to play if you ever have a jam with a sax or trumpet player. The other chords in a basic blues in B♭ are B♭7 and F7.

Eb7

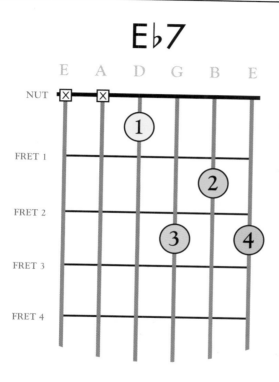

☐ = OPEN STRING ☒ = DO NOT PLAY THIS STRING ◯ = OPTIONAL NOTE

t your index finger play the 1st fret of the D string, your middle finger
e 2nd fret of the B string, your ring finger the 3rd fret of the G string
d your little finger the 3rd fret of the top E string.

173

E♭MAJOR7

This is a very useful moveable major seventh shape.
Adding the middle finger at the 3rd fret on the A string
changes it to an equally jazzy Cm9 chord.

E♭MAJOR7

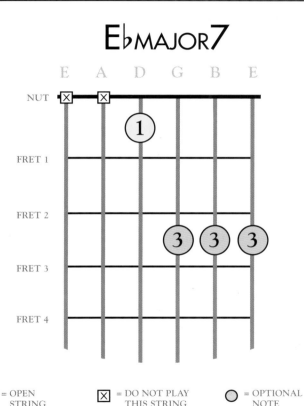

E	A	D	G	B	E

= OPEN
STRING

= DO NOT PLAY
THIS STRING

= OPTIONAL
NOTE

ing your index finger play the 1st fret of the D string, then let your ring
ger cover the 3rd fret of the top E, B and G strings.

E♭m

E♭ minor is not a guitar-friendly key, as every single open string will sound wrong! This shape takes the standard Dm shape up one fret; you can of course take any other moveable Dm shape up one fret instead.

E♭m

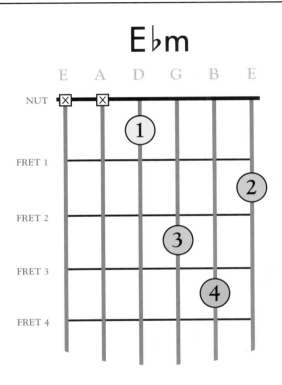

E A D G B E

NUT

FRET 1

FRET 2

FRET 3

FRET 4

1

2

3

4

◯ = OPEN STRING

⊠ = DO NOT PLAY THIS STRING

◯ = OPTIONAL NOTE

t your index finger play the 1st fret of the D string, while your middle ger plays the 2nd fret of the top E string, your ring finger the 3rd fret the G string and your little finger the 4th fret of the B string.

E♭m (alt. shape)

These moveable shapes come into their own for keys such
as E♭ minor as there really is no alternative! Try lifting
the middle finger to produce the interesting and
ambiguous chord of E♭sus2.

E♭m (alt. shape)

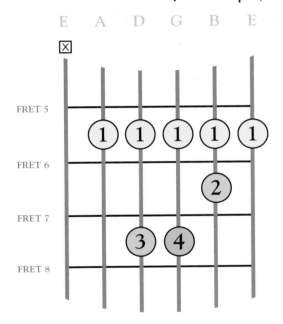

E A D G B E

FRET 5

① ① ① ① ①

FRET 6

②

FRET 7

③ ④

FRET 8

| ▣ | = OPEN STRING | ⊠ | = DO NOT PLAY THIS STRING | ◯ | = OPTIONAL NOTE |

...t your index finger play the 6th fret of the E, B, G, D and A strings,
...ur middle finger the 7th fret of the B string, your ring finger the 8th
...et of the D string and your little finger the 8th fret of the G string.

E♭m(add9)

The key of E♭ minor means that there is really no easier way
to play this chord. You can drop the barre and just play
the inner four strings if it's easier though – this sounds
absolutely fine, particularly when finger-picking.

E♭m(add9)

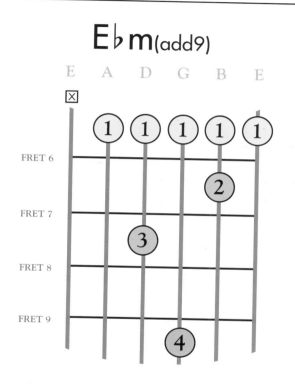

The index finger makes a barre across the A, D, G, B and top E strings at the 6th fret. The middle finger plays the B string, 7th fret. The ring finger plays the D string, 8th fret, and the little finger plays the G string, 10th fret.

E♭m7

This is the lowest available shape for this chord, based on moving the Dm7 chord up one fret. It also works as a G♭6 chord. Many players would use barre across the top E string and B string with the middle finger, and use the ring finger on the G string instead.

E♭m7

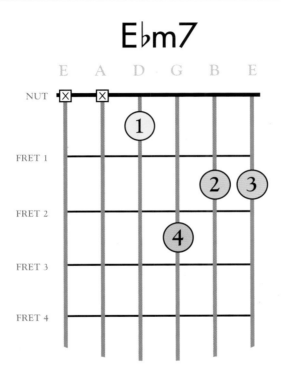

| | | | | | |
| E | A | D | G | B | E |

⊠ = OPEN STRING   ⊠ = DO NOT PLAY THIS STRING   ◯ = OPTIONAL NOTE

...sing your index finger play the 1st fret of the D string, your middle ...ger plays the 2nd fret of the B string, your ring finger the 2nd fret of ...e top E string and finally your little finger the 3rd fret of the G string.

E♭sus4

Try playing around with the suspended note in this shape
(the little finger). Bring it down a fret for a straight E♭ chord,
or lift it altogether for an E♭sus2 chord.

E♭sus4

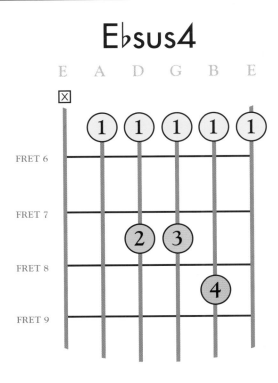

| ☐ = OPEN STRING | ☒ = DO NOT PLAY THIS STRING | ◯ = OPTIONAL NOTE |

he index finger makes a barre across the A, D, G, B and top E strings at
ne 6th fret. The middle finger plays the D string, 8th fret. The ring finger
lays the G string, 8th fret, and the little finger plays the B string, 9th fret.

E♭dim

This moveable diminished chord is very useful. Try using it as a passing chord between any kind of D chord and any kind of E chord – for example from D major to E minor.

E♭dim

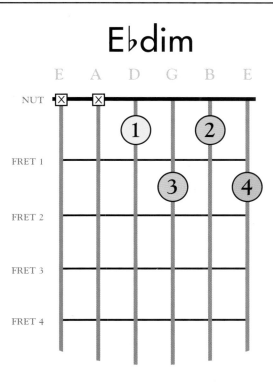

☒ = OPEN STRING   ☒ = DO NOT PLAY THIS STRING   ◯ = OPTIONAL NOTE

he index finger plays the D string, 1st fret. The middle finger plays the
string, 1st fret. The ring finger plays the G string, 2nd fret, and the little
ger plays the top E string, 2nd fret.

E

This is the daddy of all guitar chords and the second or third chord most people learn. Some interesting effects can be produced by moving this shape around the neck without a barre – try it!

E

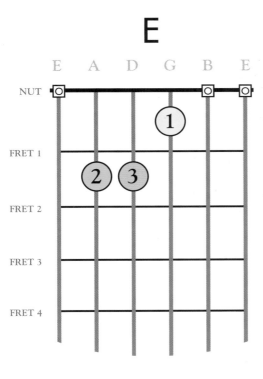

E   A   D   G   B   E

NUT

1

FRET 1

2   3

FRET 2

FRET 3

FRET 4

⊡ = OPEN STRING   ☒ = DO NOT PLAY THIS STRING   ◯ = OPTIONAL NOTE

r the E chord your index finger should play the 1st fret of the G string,
ile your middle finger plays the 2nd fret of the A string and your ring
ger the 2nd fret of the D string.

E (alt. shape)

This shape can be a little tricky; you don't actually need the bottom note in many situations – try picking just the top three strings. This can be particularly effective with light effects such as chorus.

E (alt. shape)

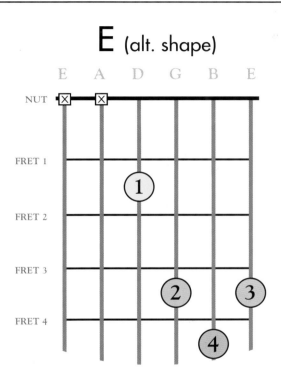

| | = OPEN STRING | | = DO NOT PLAY THIS STRING | | = OPTIONAL NOTE |

t your index finger play the 2nd fret of the D string, your middle finger
e 4th fret of the G string, your ring finger the 4th fret of the top E string
d your little finger the 5th fret of the B string.

E(add9)

This is a moody monster of a chord. Its open, confident sound can be changed completely by adding the ring finger on the B string, 3rd fret; this is quite a stretch in all, but the resulting alternative E9 shape is bound to turn heads.

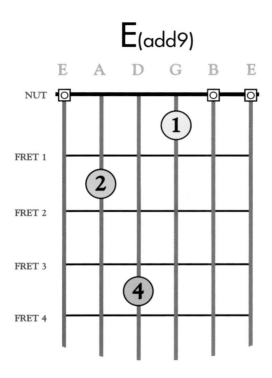

E(add9)

| = OPEN STRING | ☒ = DO NOT PLAY THIS STRING | ○ = OPTIONAL NOTE |

The index finger plays the G string, 1st fret. The middle finger plays the A string, 2nd fret and the little finger plays the D string, 4th fret. All other strings are open.

E7

The E7 chord is essential if you want to play the blues in E, which many players feel is exactly what the guitar is for. The other chords in the sequence are A7 and B7. For extra spice, add the E7(#9) 'Hendrix' chord shown on p214.

E7

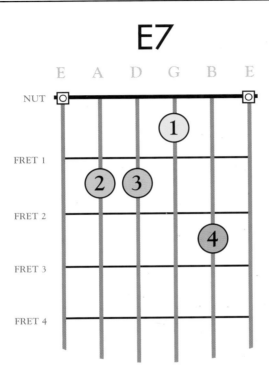

E   A   D   G   B   E

NUT

FRET 1

FRET 2

FRET 3

FRET 4

| ☐ | = OPEN STRING | ☒ | = DO NOT PLAY THIS STRING | ◯ | = OPTIONAL NOTE |

et your index finger play the 1st fret of the G string, while your middle
nger plays the 2nd fret of the A string, your ring finger the 2nd fret of
e D string and your little finger the 3rd fret of the B string.

Emajor7

This is an unusual low voicing for a major seventh chord.
Go easy on the A string – this is the note that can make the
chord sound slightly muddy. The open top E string may be
added as the note E is part of the chord, but it's
usually best left out.

EMAJOR7

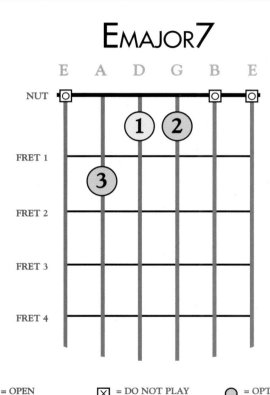

☐ = OPEN STRING   ☒ = DO NOT PLAY THIS STRING   ○ = OPTIONAL NOTE

sing your index finger play the 1st fret of the D string, while your iddle finger plays the 1st fret of the G string and finally your ring nger plays the 2nd fret of the A string.

Em

This shape is a simple and effective favourite.
Many guitar-based tunes have been written in E minor, as
there are so many opportunities for ringing open strings.
Also, you can strum this chord, leave the bottom note ringing
and add 12th-fret harmonics on the top three strings.
Always a winner!

Em

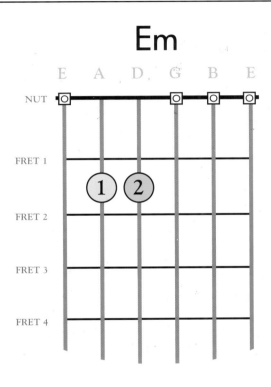

E   A   D   G   B   E

NUT

FRET 1

FRET 2

FRET 3

FRET 4

| ◯ = OPEN STRING | ☒ = DO NOT PLAY THIS STRING | ◯ = OPTIONAL NOTE |

Your index finger should play the 2nd fret of the A string, while your middle finger plays the 2nd fret of the D string. You can use the middle and ring fingers instead if that feels more comfortable.

Em (alt. shape)

This chord is twice as useful as most chords produced by moving the Am shape around with a barre, as the open low E string can be added to produce a chord voicing that is at once deep and high. Try some funky strumming on the fretted shape while letting the bottom string ring on.

Em (alt. shape)

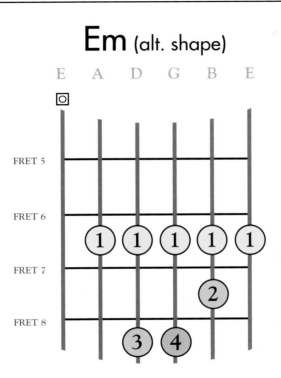

▢ = OPEN STRING	☒ = DO NOT PLAY THIS STRING
⬤ = OPTIONAL NOTE	

 your index finger play the 7th fret of the E, B, G, D and A strings, your
 ddle finger the 8th fret of the B string, your ring finger the 9th fret of
 D string and your little finger the 9th fret of the G string.

Em(add9)

This chord is a classic of gothic '80s rock.
Adding the middle finger on the B string, 3rd fret, produces
an even more mysterious voicing of the usually jazzy
Em9 chord.

Em(add9)

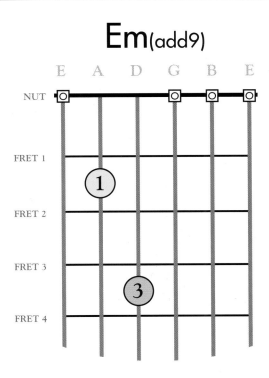

NUT

FRET 1

FRET 2

FRET 3

FRET 4

| ☐ = OPEN STRING | ☒ = DO NOT PLAY THIS STRING | ◯ = OPTIONAL NOTE |

...e index finger plays the A string, 2nd fret, and the ring finger plays the ...string, 4th fret.

Em7

This voicing of Em7 is rich and resonant. For the Oasis
'Wonderwall' version, add the little finger on the top E
string, 3rd fret. Then, if you know the song,
you'll want to shift to G…

Em7

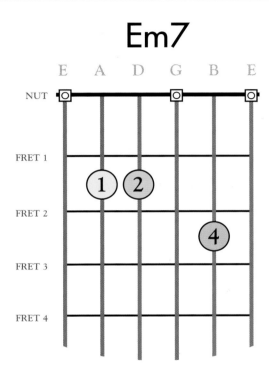

◯ = OPEN
STRING

☒ = DO NOT PLAY
THIS STRING

⬤ = OPTIONAL
NOTE

ur index finger should play the 2nd fret of the A string, while your
dle finger plays the 2nd fret of the D string and your little finger
ys the 3rd fret of the B string.

Esus4

This shape is very like an open A chord, except that the fingers are on lower strings, and it's generally best to use the middle, ring and little fingers so that the suspension can easily resolve to an E chord.

Esus4

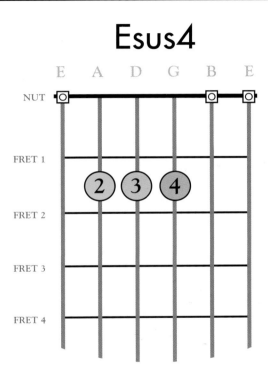

| E | A | D | G | B | E |

NUT

FRET 1

② ③ ④

FRET 2

FRET 3

FRET 4

▣ = OPEN STRING   ☒ = DO NOT PLAY THIS STRING   ⬤ = OPTIONAL NOTE

e middle finger plays the A string, the ring finger plays the D string
d the little finger plays the G string – all at the 2nd fret.

207

Edim

**This is an interesting voicing – possibly slightly muddy
if strummed but rich and sonorous if picked, particularly
with a hint of chorus or flanger.**

Edim

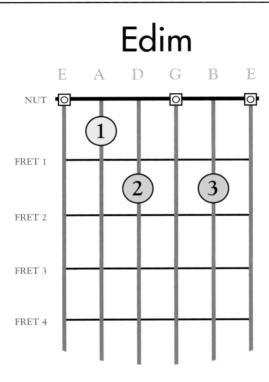

E   A   D   G   B   E

NUT

FRET 1

FRET 2

FRET 3

FRET 4

◉ = OPEN STRING   ☒ = DO NOT PLAY THIS STRING   ◯ = OPTIONAL NOTE

e index finger plays the A string, 1st fret. The middle finger plays
e D string, 2nd fret, and the ring finger plays the B string, 2nd fret.

E6

This voicing gives a full-fat version of the Beatles' favourite
ending chord – also popular with many more
recent indie/rock bands who like to tip their hats
to their '60s heroes.

E6

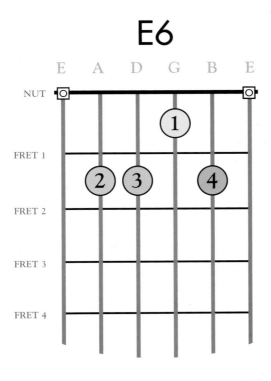

O = OPEN
STRING

X = DO NOT PLAY
THIS STRING

◯ = OPTIONAL
NOTE

et your index finger play the 1st fret of the G string, your middle finger
e 2nd fret of the A string, your ring finger plays the 2nd fret of the D
ring, and your little finger should play the 2nd fret of the B string.

E9

This slightly unusual voicing has the advantage of being fairly easy to play. Removing the ring finger reveals a very easy, and slightly more subtle, version of the E7 shape.

E9

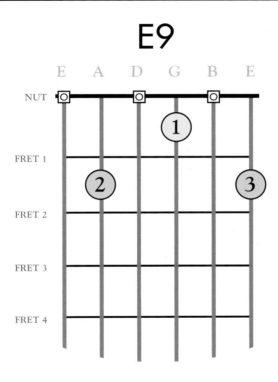

E	A	D	G	B	E

O = OPEN STRING

X = DO NOT PLAY THIS STRING

○ = OPTIONAL NOTE

sing your index finger play the 1st fret of the G string, while your
iddle finger plays the 2nd fret of the A string and your ring finger
ays the 2nd fret of the top E string.

E7#9 ('Hendrix' chord)

Though this chord is common in blues and jazz,
its use in rock is always reminiscent of Jimi Hendrix.
The shape is moveable – the root is on the A string.
In this version, the open bottom E is optional,
adding depth and force to the chord.

E7$^\sharp$9 ('Hendrix' chord)

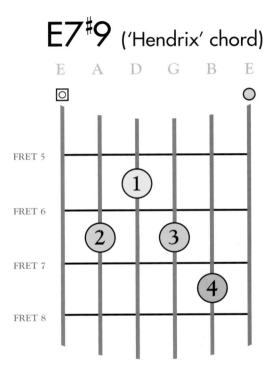

E A D G B E

FRET 5

FRET 6

FRET 7

FRET 8

| □ = OPEN STRING | ☒ = DO NOT PLAY THIS STRING | ◯ = OPTIONAL NOTE |

he index finger plays the D string, 6th fret. The middle finger plays the
 string, 7th fret. The ring finger plays the G string, 7th fret, and the little
nger plays the B string, 8th fret. The open E strings may be played.

215

F

This is basically an easier version of the F barre chord (p242)
– very useful if you haven't quite mastered the full barre
technique yet. Moving from F to B♭, as many songs in F major
do, can be made more interesting by adding the open
A string to this shape for one or two beats first.

F

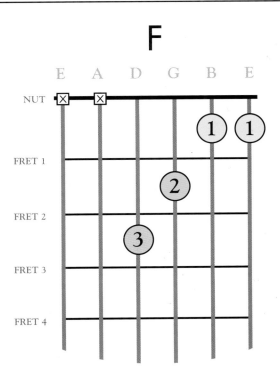

| | = OPEN STRING | | = DO NOT PLAY THIS STRING | | = OPTIONAL NOTE |

our index finger should play the 1st fret of the top E and B strings, while
our middle finger plays the 2nd fret of the G string and your ring finger
e 3rd fret of the D string.

F (alt. shape)

This unusual voicing can be turned into a nifty alternative
Dm7 shape by removing the index finger and letting the
open D string sound. Alternating between the two creates an
instant folk/country intro!

F (alt. shape)

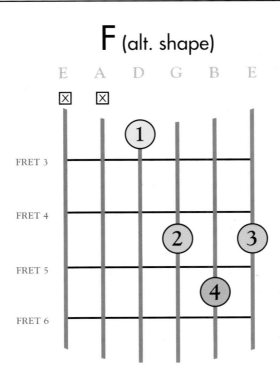

E A D G B E

FRET 3

FRET 4

FRET 5

FRET 6

| ☐ | = OPEN STRING | ☒ | = DO NOT PLAY THIS STRING | ◯ | = OPTIONAL NOTE |

...t your index finger play the 3rd fret of the D string, your middle finger
...e 5th fret of the G string, your ring finger the 5th fret of the top E string
...d your little finger the 6th fret of the B string.

F(add9)

You may find this shape very hard here, right at the bottom of the neck. One alternative is to add the little finger on the top E string, 3rd fret, to the F shape on p216, though this lacks some of the complexity of the full shape.

F(add9)

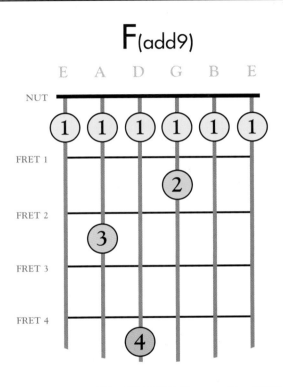

E A D G B E

NUT

FRET 1

FRET 2

FRET 3

FRET 4

⊡ = OPEN
   STRING

☒ = DO NOT PLAY
   THIS STRING

◯ = OPTIONAL
   NOTE

...he index finger makes a barre across all six strings at the 1st fret. ...e middle finger plays the G string, 2nd fret. The ring finger plays ...e A string, 3rd fret, and the little finger plays the D string, 5th fret.

F7

This shape is great for playing the blues or rock 'n' roll in F. Repeatedly hammering on from the open low E string to the 1st fret produces an easy Eddie Cochran-style riff.

F7

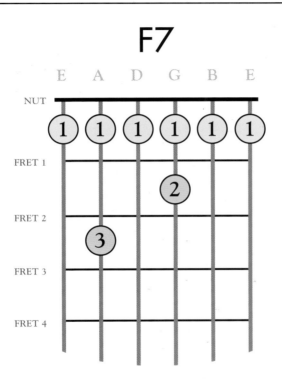

E A D G B E

NUT

FRET 1

FRET 2

FRET 3

FRET 4

◯ = OPEN STRING   ☒ = DO NOT PLAY THIS STRING   ◯ = OPTIONAL NOTE

...t your index finger play across the 1st fret of all the strings, while your ...iddle finger plays the 2nd fret of the G string and your ring finger plays ...e 3rd fret of the A string.

FMAJOR7

This is an easy shape. You may wish to use your thumb to fret the bottom E string, 1st fret, for a deeper sound; lifting the index finger to incorporate the open B string produces a complex, moody chord called Fmaj7(#11).

FMAJOR7

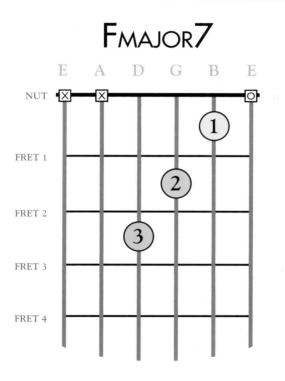

| E | A | D | G | B | E |

NUT

FRET 1

FRET 2

FRET 3

FRET 4

| ◻ = OPEN STRING | ☒ = DO NOT PLAY THIS STRING | ◯ = OPTIONAL NOTE |

ur index finger should play the 1st fret of the B string, while your
ddle finger should play the 2nd fret of the G string and your ring
ger should play the 3rd fret of the D string.

Fm

This Fm shape is based on the Dm chord.
Lifting the index finger to let the open D string
sound produces a complex jazz chord: Dm7(♭5)
(also known as a half diminished chord).

Fm

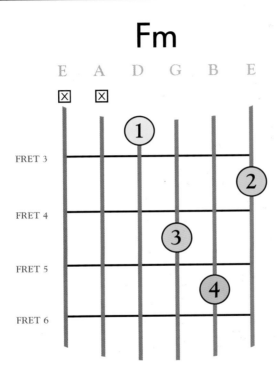

E   A   D   G   B   E

FRET 3

FRET 4

FRET 5

FRET 6

| ☐ | = OPEN STRING | ☒ | = DO NOT PLAY THIS STRING | ◯ | = OPTIONAL NOTE |

et your index finger play the 3rd fret of the D string, while your middle nger plays the 4th fret of the top E string, your ring finger the 5th fret of e G string and your little finger the 6th fret of the B string.

Fm (alt. shape)

The key of F minor has a dark and sinister sound to
some ears. Lifting the little finger from this shape produces
an easy alternative shape for Fm7.

Fm (alt. shape)

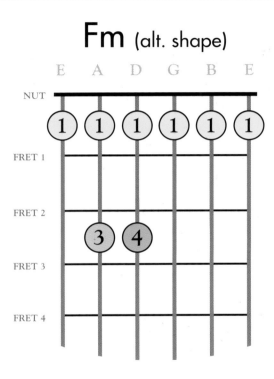

Your index finger should play the 1st fret of all the strings, while your ring finger should play the 3rd fret of the A string and your little finger should play the 3rd fret of the D string.

Fm(add9)

Ouch – this one's a stretch! If you want to play this chord
in a band, you can get away with the top four strings
(D, G, B, E) as long as the bass player plays an F.

Fm(add9)

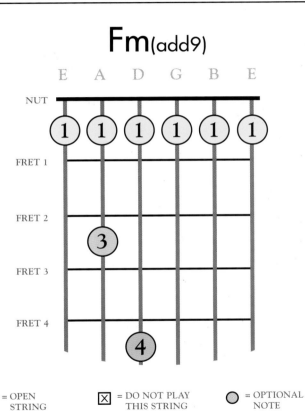

E   A   D   G   B   E

NUT

FRET 1

FRET 2

FRET 3

FRET 4

⊡ = OPEN STRING   ☒ = DO NOT PLAY THIS STRING   ◯ = OPTIONAL NOTE

The index finger makes a barre across all six strings at the 1st fret. The ring finger plays the A string, 3rd fret and the little finger plays the D string, 5th fret.

Fm7

This shape can be a bit of a handful, especially on an acoustic guitar. Remove the ring and little fingers altogether for a simpler Fm7 shape.

Fm7

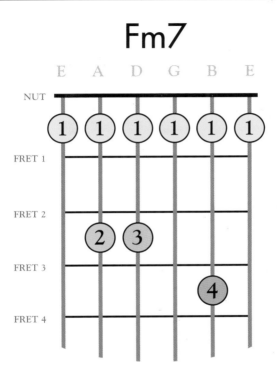

E   A   D   G   B   E

NUT

FRET 1

FRET 2

FRET 3

FRET 4

| ◎ = OPEN STRING | ☒ = DO NOT PLAY THIS STRING | ◯ = OPTIONAL NOTE |

t your index finger play the 1st fret of all the strings, your middle
ger the 3rd fret of the A string, your ring finger the 3rd fret of the
string and your little finger the 4th fret of the B string.

Fsus4

You may find it easier to play all the notes at the 3rd fret
with a barre using the ring finger – in this case either the
finger must be curved in such a way as to avoid
interfering with the top notes on the chord, or else
avoid playing the top strings.

Fsus4

E A D G B E

NUT

① ① ① ① ① ①

FRET 1

FRET 2

② ③ ④

FRET 3

FRET 4

◻ = OPEN
STRING

☒ = DO NOT PLAY
THIS STRING

◯ = OPTIONAL
NOTE

e index finger makes a barre across all six strings at the 1st fret. The
ddle, ring and little fingers play the A, D and G strings respectively,
at the 3rd fret.

Fdim

This is a particularly full voicing for a diminished chord on the guitar. This shape can be used to good effect as a rather tasteful passing chord between E and F#m.

Fdim

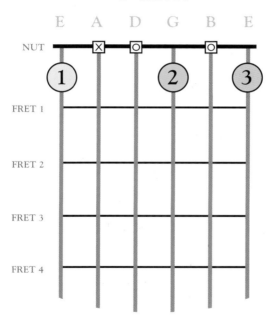

E   A   D   G   B   E

NUT

FRET 1

FRET 2

FRET 3

FRET 4

| ☐ | = OPEN STRING | ☒ | = DO NOT PLAY THIS STRING | ◯ | = OPTIONAL NOTE |

e index finger plays the bottom E string, 1st fret. The middle finger
ys the G string, 1st fret and the ring finger plays the top E string,
fret. The D and B strings are open; the A string is not played.

F6

This is an easy F6 shape which can also double as B♭maj7
or Dm. For a fuller version, add the low E string,
1st fret, with your thumb.

F6

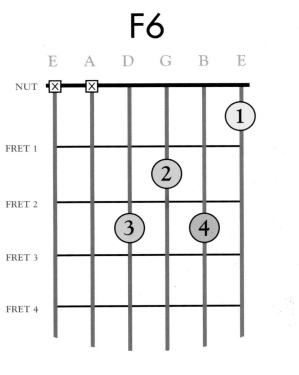

E   A   D   G   B   E

NUT

FRET 1

FRET 2

FRET 3

FRET 4

⬛ = OPEN STRING   ☒ = DO NOT PLAY THIS STRING   ⬤ = OPTIONAL NOTE

ʊur index finger should play the 1st fret of the top E string, your middle ₅ger the 2nd fret of the G string, your ring finger the 3rd fret of the D ₅ing and your little finger the 3rd fret of the B string.

F9

Lifting the little finger from this shape results in a
standard F7 shape. The little finger can also be moved
up by one fret to produce an F7(#9) chord.

F9

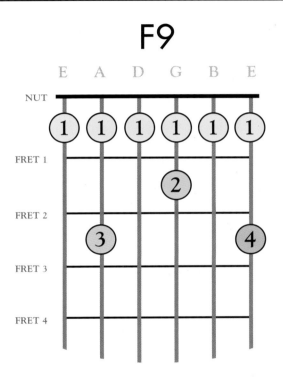

E   A   D   G   B   E

NUT

FRET 1

FRET 2

FRET 3

FRET 4

☐ = OPEN
STRING

☒ = DO NOT PLAY
THIS STRING

◯ = OPTIONAL
NOTE

...t your index finger play the 1st fret of all six strings, your middle finger
...e 2nd fret of the G string, your ring finger the 3rd fret of the A string
...d your little finger the 3rd fret of the top E string.

F barre

This is the first barre chord many players learn –
once the basic technique is mastered, the whole fretboard
is at your disposal. Now try removing the barre –
this produces a rich and complex Spanish-sounding
chord with no agreed name!

F barre

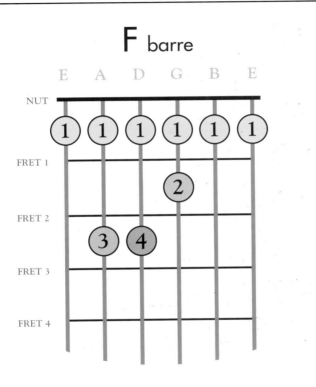

☐ = OPEN STRING

☒ = DO NOT PLAY THIS STRING

◯ = OPTIONAL NOTE

...et your index finger play the 1st fret of all the strings, while your middle ...nger plays the 2nd fret of the G string, your ring finger the 3rd fret of ...he A string and your little finger the 3rd fret of the D string.

F#

This F# major shape is essentially an easy version of the full barre chord shape – simply extend the index finger barre across all six strings to play this. Letting the top E string sound open instead produces an alternative F#7 chord.

F#

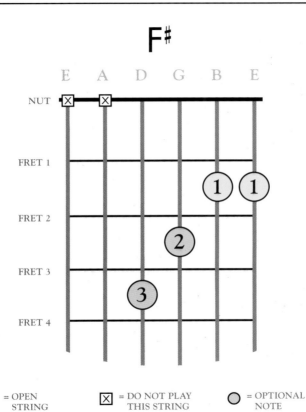

☐ = OPEN
STRING

☒ = DO NOT PLAY
THIS STRING

⬤ = OPTIONAL
NOTE

For the F# chord use your index finger to play the 2nd fret of the top E and B strings, while your middle finger plays the 3rd fret of the G string and your ring finger plays the 4th fret of the D string.

F[#] (alt. shape)

The lowest note can often be omitted from this shape, especially if playing with a band. If so, you may want to use fingers 1, 2 and 3 in order to be able to use the little finger to add a suspended 4th (see Dsus4, p158).

F# (alt. shape)

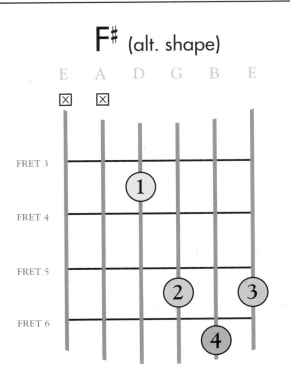

| ☒ = OPEN STRING | ☒ = DO NOT PLAY THIS STRING | ◯ = OPTIONAL NOTE |

Let your index finger play the 4th fret of the D string, your middle finger the 6th fret of the G string, your ring finger the 6th fret of the top E string and your little finger the 7th fret of the B string.

247

F#(add9)

This full barre chord is a bit of a stretch at the 2nd fret.
Picking this chord can actually be easier than strumming,
simply because one can concentrate on making sure each
individual note sounds well.

F#(add9)

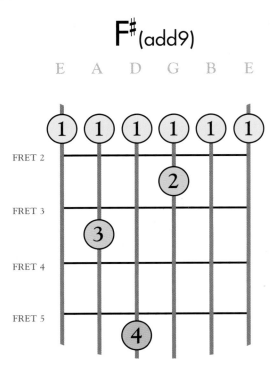

E   A   D   G   B   E

FRET 2

FRET 3

FRET 4

FRET 5

◻ = OPEN
STRING

☒ = DO NOT PLAY
THIS STRING

◯ = OPTIONAL
NOTE

...e index finger makes a barre across all six strings at the 2nd fret.
...e middle finger plays the G string, 3rd fret. The ring finger plays the
...string, 4th fret, and the little finger plays the D string, 6th fret.

F#7

Seventh chords are very useful in blues or
jazz and also make very effective 'pivot' chords.
Try the sequence D – G – F#7 – Bm: can you hear how
the F#7 signals the key change?

F#7

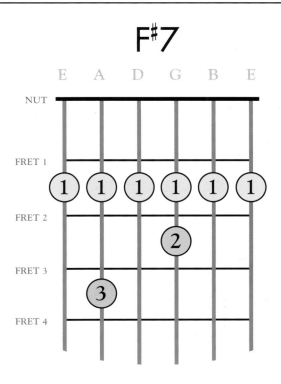

E   A   D   G   B   E

NUT

FRET 1

FRET 2

FRET 3

FRET 4

⊡ = OPEN
STRING

☒ = DO NOT PLAY
THIS STRING

⬤ = OPTIONAL
NOTE

et your index finger play across the 2nd fret of all the strings, while
ur middle finger plays the 3rd fret of the G string and your ring finger
ays the 4th fret of the A string.

251

F#MAJOR7

This is another shape that's very easy to remember.
The bottom note can be omitted if you're playing with a
band, in which case the chord can be embellished by moving
the little finger to the top E string, 4th fret.

F#MAJOR7

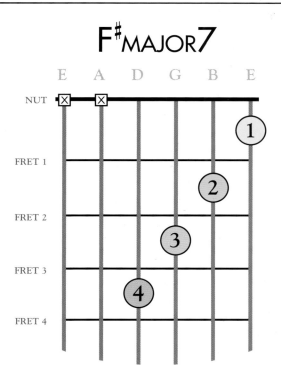

| O | = OPEN STRING | X | = DO NOT PLAY THIS STRING | ⬤ | = OPTIONAL NOTE |

...t your index finger play the 1st fret of the top E string, your middle ...ger the 2nd fret of the B string, your ring finger the 3rd fret of the ...string and your little finger the 4th fret of the D string.

F#m

The chord of F#m is an important one in the keys
of A and D major. Try these sequences: A – F#m – Bm — E7
and D – F#m – G – A7.

F#m

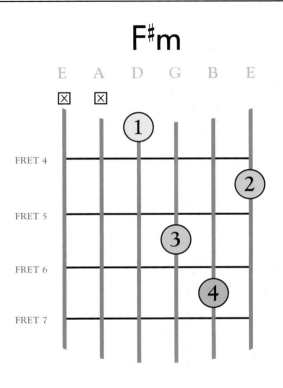

| E | A | D | G | B | E |

☒ = OPEN STRING

☒ = DO NOT PLAY THIS STRING

◯ = OPTIONAL NOTE

et your index finger play the 4th fret of the D string, your middle finger
e 5th fret of the top E string, your ring finger the 6th fret of the G string
d your little finger the 7th fret of the B string.

255

F#m (alt. shape)

This fully moveable barre shape produces an F#m
at the 2nd fret. You may want to use just the top four strings
if playing with a band or another guitarist; try adding the
open A string for a couple of beats if the next chord is Bm.

F#m (alt. shape)

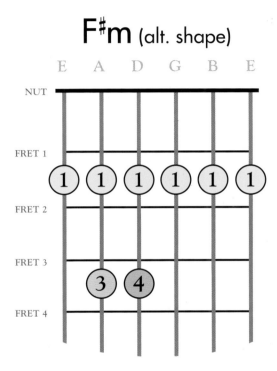

E	A	D	G	B	E

◯ = OPEN STRING   ⊠ = DO NOT PLAY THIS STRING   ◯ = OPTIONAL NOTE

sing your index finger play the 2nd fret of all six strings. Your ring finger
ould play the 4th fret of the A string and your little finger should play
e 4th fret of the D string.

F#m(add9)

This chord can spice up any sequence in
A major or F# minor. Adding a ninth to one chord in a
sequence often results in a temptation to add it to
all the rest. Do you recognise the following sequence?
A(add9) – F#m(add9) – D(add9) – E(add9).
(The Police: 'Every Breath You Take').

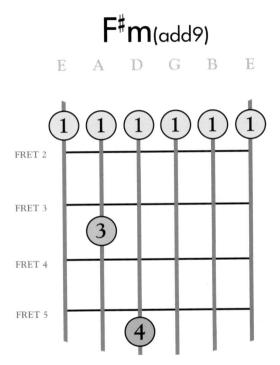

F#m(add9)

E A D G B E

FRET 2

FRET 3

FRET 4

FRET 5

☐ = OPEN STRING ☒ = DO NOT PLAY THIS STRING ⬤ = OPTIONAL NOTE

The index finger makes a barre across all six strings at the 2nd fret.
The ring finger plays the A string, 4th fret, and the little finger plays
the D string, 6th fret.

F#m7

This very jazzy chord voicing can be turned into something classical by simply lifting the index finger to produce a second inversion A/E chord. Try the sequence:
F#m – A/E – E7 – A.

F#m7

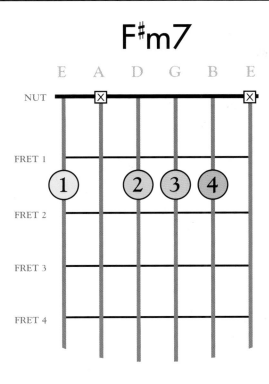

◯ = OPEN
STRING

☒ = DO NOT PLAY
THIS STRING

◯ = OPTIONAL
NOTE

Let your index finger play the 2nd fret of the bottom E string, your middle finger the 2nd fret of the D string, your ring finger the 2nd fret of the G string and your little finger the 2nd fret of the B string.

F[#]sus4

F#sus4 sounds as though it wants to resolve to a
straight F# chord, but denying this expectation can create
a string sequence. Try a descending sequence of
sus4 chords with a delayed resolution:
F#sus4 – Esus4 – Dsus4 – C#sus4 – C# – F#.

F#sus4

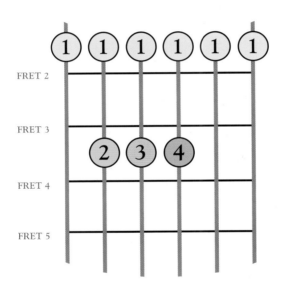

☐ = OPEN
STRING

☒ = DO NOT PLAY
THIS STRING

◯ = OPTIONAL
NOTE

The index finger makes a barre across all six strings at the 2nd fret. The middle, ring and little fingers play the A, D and G strings respectively, all at the 4th fret.

F#dim

This diminished voicing makes a great passing chord.
Try it between Fmaj7 and Gm7 – many a classic
Latin jazz song does just this.

F#dim

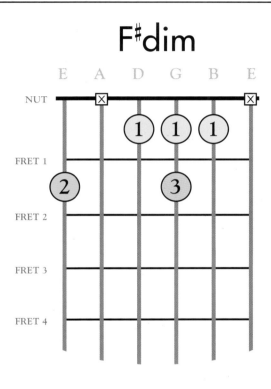

☐ = OPEN STRING   ☒ = DO NOT PLAY THIS STRING   ⬤ = OPTIONAL NOTE

he index finger makes a half barre across the D, G and B strings at the
st fret. The index finger plays the low E string, 2nd fret, and the ring
ger plays the G string, 2nd fret. The A and top E strings are not played.

G

This chord belongs among the really important shapes,
especially on acoustic guitar. Some beginners find it
a little tricky – using fingers 1, 2 and 3 in the same order
is a valid alternative.

G

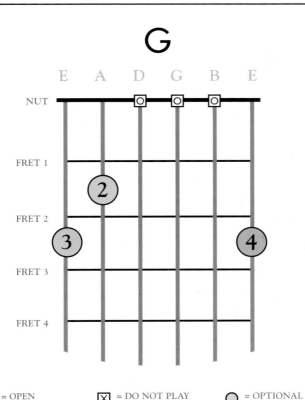

| ☐ = OPEN STRING | ☒ = DO NOT PLAY THIS STRING | ◯ = OPTIONAL NOTE |

ɔr the G chord your middle finger should play the 2nd fret of the A
ɾing, while your ring finger plays the 3rd fret of the bottom E string
ʌd your little finger plays the 3rd fret of the top E string.

G (alt. shape)

This version of the G shape gives a slightly stronger, more 'rock' sound. There are many easy possibilities when playing this chord: lift the middle finger for an alternative Em7 shape, or lift the little finger for an interesting voicing for G6.

G (alt. shape)

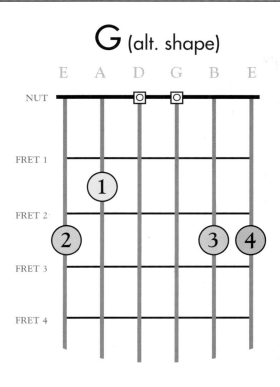

| E | A | D | G | B | E |

| = OPEN STRING | = DO NOT PLAY THIS STRING | = OPTIONAL NOTE |

...et your index finger play the 2nd fret of the A string, your middle finger ...e 3rd fret of the bottom E, your ring finger the 3rd fret of the B string ...d your little finger the 3rd fret of the top E.

G(add9)

For once, an 'add9' chord that doesn't involve a huge stretch!
This one instantly sounds like James Taylor; try hammering
on and pulling off with the index finger – you can also
do this on the D string, 2nd fret.

G(add9)

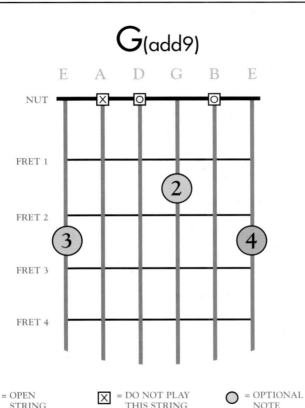

| = OPEN STRING | ☒ = DO NOT PLAY THIS STRING | ⬤ = OPTIONAL NOTE |

he middle finger plays the G string, 2nd fret. The ring finger plays the
w E string, 3rd fret and the little finger plays the top E string, 3rd fret.
he D and B strings are open; the A string is not played.

G7

G7 is actually an easier shape than the straight G chords
and adds spice to the key of C major. Try this sequence:
Am7 – D7 – G7 – C. Do you recognise it?
(The Beatles: 'Rocky Raccoon').

G7

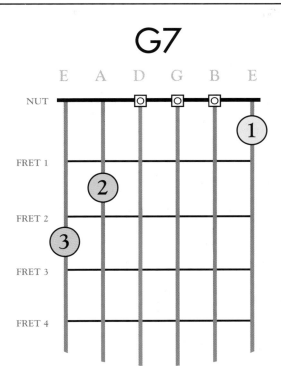

E A D G B E

NUT

FRET 1

FRET 2

FRET 3

FRET 4

| ☐ | = OPEN STRING | ☒ | = DO NOT PLAY THIS STRING | ○ | = OPTIONAL NOTE |

our index finger should play the 1st fret of the top E string,
our middle finger should play the 2nd fret of the A string
nd your ring finger should play the 3rd fret of the bottom E string.

273

GMAJOR7

This lovely sounding chord can be substituted for the
G chord in many situations when playing songs in the key
of D or G. The sequence G – Gmaj7 – G7 is an easy pop
favourite, usually resolving to a C major chord.

Gmajor7

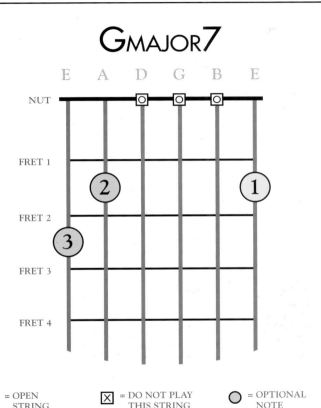

E A D G B E

NUT

FRET 1

FRET 2

FRET 3

FRET 4

☐ = OPEN STRING   ☒ = DO NOT PLAY THIS STRING   ⬤ = OPTIONAL NOTE

Use your index finger to play the 2nd fret of the top E string, while your middle finger plays the 2nd fret of the A string and your ring finger plays the 3rd fret of the bottom E string.

275

Gm

This Gm chord is based on the Dm shape, but it's good to
know that the top three notes are very useful on their own,
functioning well as an E♭maj7 or B♭6 if playing with a bass
player or second guitar.

Gm

E A D G B E

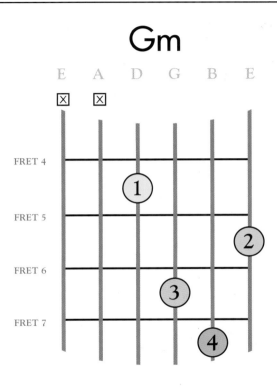

FRET 4

① 1

FRET 5

② 2

FRET 6

③ 3

FRET 7

④ 4

| ⊡ = OPEN STRING | ☒ = DO NOT PLAY THIS STRING | ◯ = OPTIONAL NOTE |

Let your index finger play the 5th fret of the D string, while your middle finger plays the 6th fret of the top E string, your ring finger the 7th fret of the G string and your little finger the 8th fret of the B string.

Gm (alt. shape)

This full barre chord is usually the best choice for Gm near
the bottom of the fretboard. Don't forget that playing the
bottom three strings results in a power chord that
generally sounds better than the full chord if you're
playing with distortion.

Gm (alt. shape)

E A D G B E

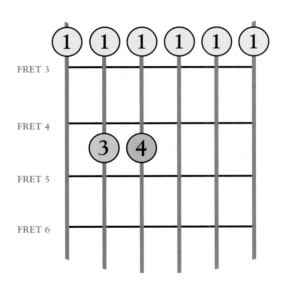

FRET 3

FRET 4

FRET 5

FRET 6

◻ = OPEN
STRING

☒ = DO NOT PLAY
THIS STRING

◯ = OPTIONAL
NOTE

Using your index finger play the 3rd fret of all six strings,
while your ring finger should play the 5th fret of the A string
and your little finger should play the 5th fret of the D string.

Gm(add9)

This shape is based on the Gm barre chord – just move the little finger up two frets. If this is a bit of a stretch, you can usually get away with just the top four strings, particularly if you're playing with a bass player.

Gm(add9)

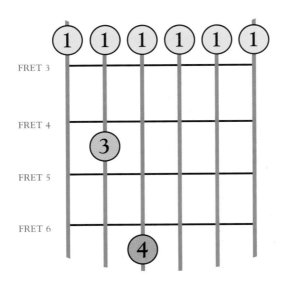

E   A   D   G   B   E

⬜ = OPEN STRING   ⊠ = DO NOT PLAY THIS STRING   ⬤ = OPTIONAL NOTE

The index finger makes a barre across all six strings at the 3rd fret.
The ring finger plays the A string, 5th fret, and the little finger plays
the D string, 7th fret.

Gm7

This Gm7 shape is a jazz voicing. Be careful not to let the
A or top E strings sound. This shape works particularly well
in Latin jazz – try playing a Bossa Nova rhythm.

Gm7

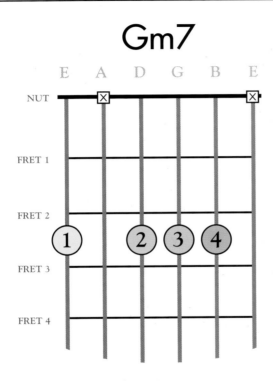

☐ = OPEN STRING   ☒ = DO NOT PLAY THIS STRING   ⬤ = OPTIONAL NOTE

et your index finger play the 3rd fret of the bottom E string,
our middle finger the 3rd fret of the D string, your ring finger the 3rd
et of the G string and your little finger the 3rd fret of the B string.

Gsus4

Sus chords are so distinctive that many songs have been
written around them, such as The Who's 'Pinball Wizard'.
This Gsus4 is an easy shape – be careful not to let the A
string sound or it will get rather muddy. You may want to
mute it with the side of your ring finger.

Gsus4

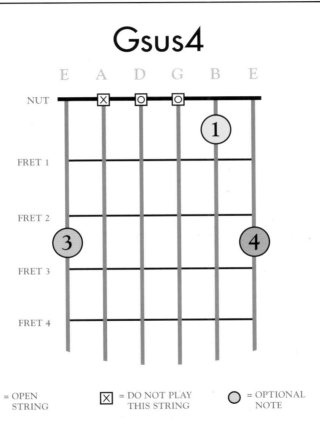

E	A	D	G	B	E

⊡ = OPEN STRING ☒ = DO NOT PLAY THIS STRING ⬤ = OPTIONAL NOTE

he index finger plays the B string, 1st fret. The ring finger plays the
ow E string, 3rd fret, and the little finger plays the top E string, 3rd fret.
he D and G strings are played open; the A string is not played.

Gdim

This chord can be played in many different places.
Try adding the little finger on the top E string, 3rd fret, for a
fuller sound; this chord makes an excellent passing chord –
try it between Fm and A♭.

Gdim

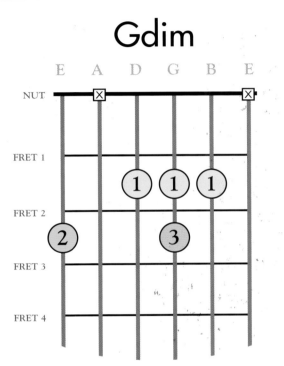

E   A   D   G   B   E

NUT

FRET 1

FRET 2

FRET 3

FRET 4

| ⃞○ | = OPEN STRING | ⃞✕ | = DO NOT PLAY THIS STRING | ⬤ | = OPTIONAL NOTE |

'he index finger makes a half barre across the 2nd fret of the D, G and B
trings. The middle finger plays the low E string, 3rd fret, and the ring
nger plays the G string, 3rd fret. The A and top E strings are not played.

G6

This useful voicing for G6 can also serve as a Cmaj7 or Em
if you're working with a bass player. For a stronger G sound
when playing alone, try adding the E string, 3rd fret –
you'll need to wrap your thumb over for this.

G6

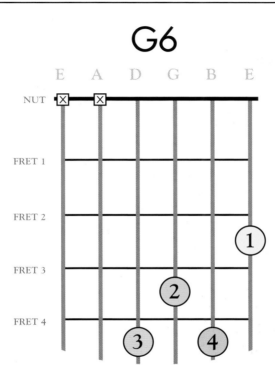

☐ = OPEN STRING   ☒ = DO NOT PLAY THIS STRING   ○ = OPTIONAL NOTE

Let your index finger play the 3rd fret of the top E string, while your middle finger plays the 4th fret of the G string, your ring finger the 5th fret of the D string and your little finger the 5th fret of the B string.

G9

This is a full, if slightly unusual, voicing for a dominant
ninth chord. Removing the little finger reveals a moveable
seventh shape – G7 at this fret. The ninth chord can also
be turned into a G7#9 by moving the
little finger to the 6th fret.

G9

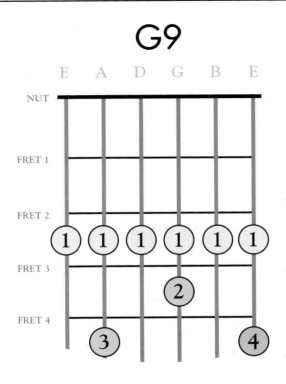

E   A   D   G   B   E

NUT

FRET 1

FRET 2

FRET 3

FRET 4

◻ = OPEN STRING ⊠ = DO NOT PLAY THIS STRING ◯ = OPTIONAL NOTE

Let your index finger play the 3rd fret of all six strings, your middle finger the 4th fret of the G string, your ring finger the 5th fret of the A string and your little finger the 5th fret of the top E string.

291

G barre

Though open G shapes are among most acoustic players'
favourite shapes, don't overlook the barre chord version:
it's a little brighter and clearer as a whole, and excellent for
rock rhythm work – try it with occasional left-hand damping.

G barre

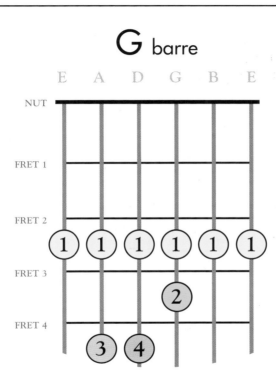

E   A   D   G   B   E

NUT

FRET 1

FRET 2

FRET 3

FRET 4

☐ = OPEN STRING   ☒ = DO NOT PLAY THIS STRING   ◯ = OPTIONAL NOTE

Let your index finger play the 3rd fret of every string, your middle finger the 4th fret of the G string, your ring finger the 5th fret of the A string and your little finger the 5th fret of the D string.

A♭

This shape can be seen as the top half of a full E-shape barre
chord. Be careful not to strike the bottom two strings when
playing this shape as the result will be very dissonant – for
this reason many players would mute them by wrapping
their thumb over the neck.

A♭

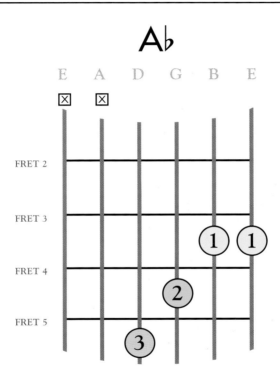

= OPEN STRING

= DO NOT PLAY THIS STRING

= OPTIONAL NOTE

To play the chord of A flat, let your index finger play the 4th frets of the B and top E strings, your middle finger play the 5th fret of the G string and your ring finger play the 6th fret of the D string.

A♭ (alt. shape)

This is an interesting, slightly tricky shape. It is basically a
D shape moved up the neck; because of the way all the
fingers are used, there is little room for embellishment,
however, so this shape remains little used.

A♭(alt. shape)

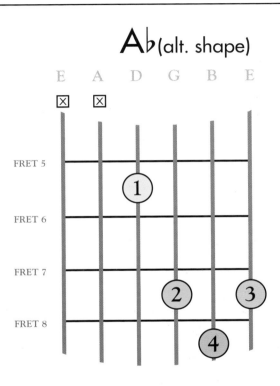

☒ = OPEN STRING   ☒ = DO NOT PLAY THIS STRING   ◯ = OPTIONAL NOTE

Let your index finger play the 6th fret of the D string, your middle finger the 8th fret of the G string, your ring finger the 8th fret of the top E string and your little finger the 9th fret of the B string.

A♭(add9)

This shape sounds great when played in full, but the
lowest three notes are actually the most important.
Try arpeggiating just the lowest three notes of a series
of 'add9' chords – the result may well remind you of the
Police classic 'Message In a Bottle'.

Ab(add9)

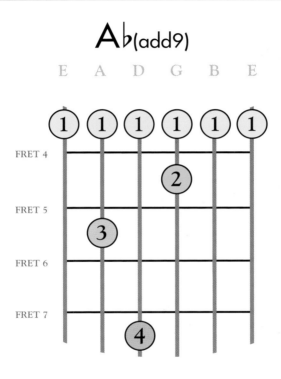

The index finger makes a barre across all six strings at the 4th fret. The middle finger plays the G string, 5th fret. The ring finger plays the A string, 6th fret, and the little finger plays the D string, 8th fret.

A♭7

This moveable chord is one of the most useful shapes in any guitarist's repertoire – not just in A♭! Try adding the little finger on the A string, 8th fret. Rocking back and forth between this and the basic shape is known as the 'Chuck Berry Boogie' – a basic rock 'n' roll pattern.

Ab7

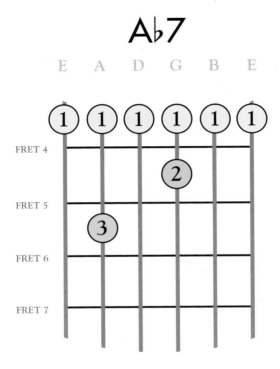

E	A	D	G	B	E

☐ = OPEN STRING

☒ = DO NOT PLAY THIS STRING

⬤ = OPTIONAL NOTE

Let your index finger play across the 4th frets of all the strings, while your middle finger plays the 5th fret of the G string and your ring finger plays the 6th fret of the A string.

301

A♭MAJOR7

This is another almost pianistic voicing that is great for disco and soul patterns. In a band context, you don't even need the root note – try playing just the top three strings and sliding up or down one fret at a time.

A♭MAJOR7

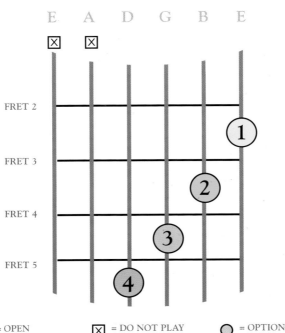

☒ = OPEN STRING

☒ = DO NOT PLAY THIS STRING

◯ = OPTIONAL NOTE

The index finger plays the top E string, 3rd fret. The middle finger plays the B string, 4th fret. The ring finger plays the G string, 5th fret, and the little finger plays the D string, 6th fret.

303

A♭m

This moveable shape is essentially Dm
moved up the neck, and is rather useful,
though generally under-used.

A♭m

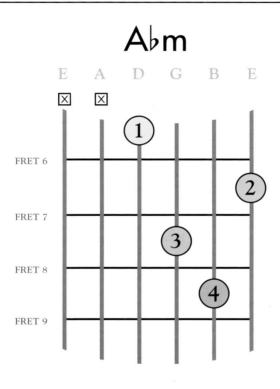

E   A   D   G   B   E

FRET 6

FRET 7

FRET 8

FRET 9

⊙ = OPEN STRING	☒ = DO NOT PLAY THIS STRING	◯ = OPTIONAL NOTE

Let your index finger play the 6th fret of the D string, your middle finger the 7th fret of the top E string, your ring finger the 8th fret of the G string and your little finger the 9th fret of the B string.

305

A♭m (alt. shape)

This is the full barre chord version. Lifting the little finger produces an alternative A♭m7 shape; shifting it to the top E string, 6th fret, results in the even jazzier A♭m9.

A♭m (alt. shape)

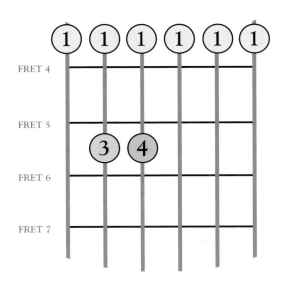

E   A   D   G   B   E

☐ = OPEN STRING   ☒ = DO NOT PLAY THIS STRING   ◯ = OPTIONAL NOTE

Use your index finger to play across all six strings at the 4th fret.
Let your ring finger play the 6th fret of the A string and your little finger
play the 6th fret of the D string.

307

A♭m(add9)

If you find this shape too much of a stretch, try it at a higher
fret first – for example, moving the barre to the 10th fret
produces a D(add9). Work this into your practice and
bring it down the neck one fret at a time until you
can play it anywhere.

A♭m(add9)

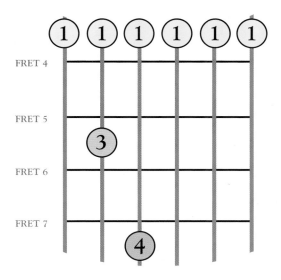

E   A   D   G   B   E

FRET 4

FRET 5

FRET 6

FRET 7

⊡ = OPEN
STRING

⊠ = DO NOT PLAY
THIS STRING

◯ = OPTIONAL
NOTE

The index finger makes a barre across all six strings at the 4th fret.
The ring finger plays the A string, 6th fret, and the little finger plays the
D string, 8th fret.

A♭m7

This is a full, resonant voicing for the A♭m7 chord.
Bringing the little finger down to the 6th fret produces a
jazzy minor sixth chord – great for sophisticated ballads.

THE Ab CHORD FAMILY

Abm7

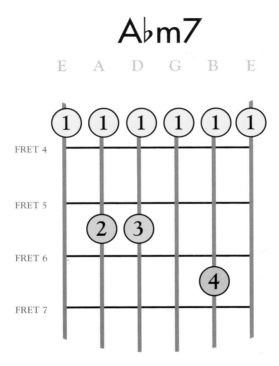

E   A   D   G   B   E

FRET 4

FRET 5

FRET 6

FRET 7

☐ = OPEN STRING   ☒ = DO NOT PLAY THIS STRING   ◯ = OPTIONAL NOTE

Let your index finger play across the 4th fret of every string, while your middle finger plays the 6th fret of the A string, your ring finger the 6th fret of the D string and your little finger the 7th fret of the B string.

A♭sus4

Lifting the ring finger from this shape results in an A♭7sus4
chord, though you may find it more natural to use
fingers 1, 3 and 4 to play this, so it can easily
resolve to A♭7 (see p300).

A♭sus4

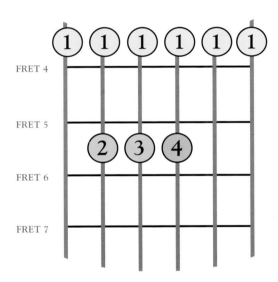

| = OPEN STRING | ⊠ = DO NOT PLAY THIS STRING | ⬤ = OPTIONAL NOTE |

The index finger makes a barre across all six strings at the 4th fret. The middle, ring and little fingers play the A, D and G strings respectively, all at the 6th fret.

A♭dim

Diminished chords can be used in so many different ways.
This one makes an excellent choice as a passing chord
between any G chord (major, minor, seventh etc.)
and any A chord.

A♭dim

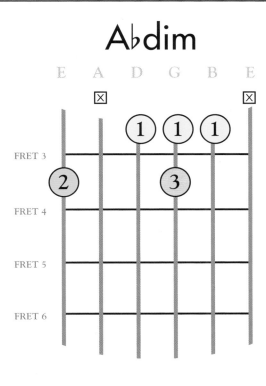

E   A   D   G   B   E

FRET 3

FRET 4

FRET 5

FRET 6

| ☐ | = OPEN STRING | ☒ | = DO NOT PLAY THIS STRING | ◯ | = OPTIONAL NOTE |

The index finger makes a half barre across the D, G and B strings at the 3rd fret. The middle finger plays the low E string, 4th fret, and the ring finger plays the G string, 4th fret. The A and top E strings are not played.

Glossary

Arpeggio
The notes in a chord played one at a time.

Bar
A subdivision of time in music.

Barre
The use of your index finger to hold down more than one string at one fret in a single chord, in order to build chords using that fret as the 'nut'.

Barre chord
A guitar chord in which your index finger barres all strings at one fret, and the rest of the chord is built using that fret as the nut. For example, in an F sharp chord, the index finger barres the second fret, and the other three fingers make an E chord, using the second fret as the nut.

Body
The main part of a guitar (not the neck).

Bridge
The bridge is located on the body of the guitar and transfers sound from the strings to the body of the guitar. This can be held in place by screws or string tension.

Chord
Three or more pitches played simultaneously, usually a root, third, and fifth, though sometimes a seventh is added.

Diminished chord
A chord consisting of a minor third and a diminished fifth. For example, a D diminished chord contains D, F and A flat.

Electric guitar
A guitar that can be electrically amplified (usually with a solid body).

Flats
Flat generally just means lower. The flat of the note you are on would be one semitone lower. To tune flat, you tune 'down'.

Fret
Technically, the frets are the small metal bars across the neck of your guitar or bass. When you press your fingertip down between two 'frets', you will fret the string and make the appropriate corresponding note. (you do not press your fingertip 'on' the frets, but between them).

Harmony
Two or more notes sounding simultaneously.

Melody

A succession of musical notes played one after another (usually the most recognizable tune of a song).

Major

This is a type of scale or chord that sounds bright, happier and more upbeat. It has no flats in it.

Minor

This is a type of scale or chord that sounds darker, maybe more sad and gloomy. Minor scales or chords do use flats.

Neck

The part of a guitar that houses the fret board.

Position

The four frets that your hand is over at any given time. 'Position' also refers to the pattern of notes to be played at any four frets for your chosen scale.

Open

A string played with no left hand fingers fretting any note.

Open chord

A chord that contains open strings.

Pick

A small, triangular-shaped piece of plastic used for striking the guitar strings with the right hand.

Rhythm

A sequence of events played with the right hand on a guitar, which gives a piece of music a distinct beat.

Scale

A group of notes that work well together.

Sharps

Sharp generally just means higher. The sharp of the note you are on would be one semitone higher. To tune sharp, you tune 'up'.

Strap

Used to hold the guitar while in standing position.

Strumming

A technique where the right hand plays the noted of a chord simultaneously, either with down or up strokes.

Swing

A rhythm in music in which the downbeat is felt slightly longer than the upbeat (sometimes called a shuffle).

Tempo

The speed of a piece of music.

Index